P9-CMW-293

# EASY VEGAN BREAKFASTS & LUNCHES

# EASY VEGAN BREAKFASTS & LUNCHES

## The Best Way to Eat Plant-Based Meals On the Go

## Maya Sozer

### Chef & founder of Dreamy Leaf

PAGE STREET
PUBLISHING CO.

Copyright © 2016 Maya Sozer

First published in 2016 by

Page Street Publishing Co.

27 Congress Street, Suite 103

Salem, MA 01970

www.pagestreetpublishing.com

All rights reserved. No part of this book may be reproduced or used, in any form or by any means, electronic or mechanical, without prior permission in writing from the publisher.

Distributed by Macmillan, sales in Canada by The Canadian Manda Group.

19  18  17  16     2  3  4  5  6

ISBN-13: 9781624142635

ISBN-10: 162414263X

Library of Congress Control Number: 2016934576

Cover and book design by Page Street Publishing Co.

Photography by Maya Sozer

Printed and bound in China

Page Street is proud to be a member of 1% for the Planet. Members donate one percent of their sales to one or more of the over 1,500 environmental and sustainability charities across the globe who participate in this program.

Dedicated to all those who get to read this, who love home cooking, who care about the health and well-being of their own, of the animals and of the environment. Thank you for exploring plant-based foods.

# CONTENTS

# INTRODUCTION

Every time you pick up this book, I smile a little.

Whether you are a vegan or not makes no difference here. You may be seeking kinder, cruelty-free foods, a more sustainable diet or improved health through nutrition and nourishment. Regardless of your interest, I am so happy you prefer or are considering plant-based foods. And I hope you will find this book a good resource.

Most chefs would agree that the taste of a dish is not proportional to the complexity of the recipe. What produces a magical taste is not usually elaborate and long-drawn-out kitchen processes; rather, novel ideas and the right combination of basic ingredients while keeping an eye on the aesthetics and textural aspects. So, it is entirely possible to cook absolutely delicious meals daily without having to live permanently in the kitchen.

Culinary motivations aside, cooking your own meals is also one the best gifts you can reward yourself or your family with. Together with the enormous investment you make in your health by having home-cooked meals, you get to enjoy the highest-quality food for the money spent.

This book is written, in part, to convince you that cooking your meals yourself, day in and day out, doesn't have to be a daunting task. Time being the chief argument against home cooking, this book strives to minimize the effort and complexity of the recipes. It focuses specifically on vegan breakfast and lunch options with a great emphasis on simplicity, portability and ultimately the wholesome, nutritious deliciousness that will feed your body and senses.

A note on gluten: I don't personally follow a strict gluten-free diet. But a large majority of the recipes included here are gluten-free or adaptable to a gluten-free diet.

Breakfast, with the apt reputation as the most important meal of the day, will hopefully stop being another morning chore often skipped but will instead become something to look forward to, something to wake up to. After all, the morning sets the mood for the day, and it helps brighten it up a little by treating ourselves to a good breakfast without turning it into a hassle. Hopefully, the thin line between is managed well in the breakfast recipes included here.

I have high expectations from lunch, and I know that you do, too. By lunchtime, I am tired and I need to be refreshed, reenergized, stimulated, comforted and pampered. A lot is expected from just a meal, but such is the task of the lunch as I see it. It is really tempting to go out for lunch or to frozen-meal our way through it, for obvious reasons. Both of those options have well-known drawbacks, but I am more interested in addressing the drawbacks of home cooking our lunches. Thus the recipes for lunch are generally conceived to be the make-ahead type. They are easy, as the title suggests, they are portable and they strive to meet the high standards set for a good lunch.

Breakfast and lunch are really two distinct meals, but we all know that the lines between the meals can get fuzzy in real life. So, this book will arm you with snack options and vegan basics to enable you to handle the cravings and create your own recipes.

There are two kitchen items that I highly recommend you invest in: a good-quality food processor and a high-speed blender. They are the two magical pieces of equipment that most recipes rely on for your ease. Besides the equipment, I suggest you consider spices as your best friends in the kitchen. Have them ready and don't hesitate to experiment. They are transformative.

In the age of connectivity, a book like this does not represent a far-removed author who only lives in the realm of the book pages. I am real and accessible to you. The recipes here are developed and tested as tediously as could be afforded, but no instruction is perfect, and I fully expect to have made mistakes despite my best efforts to minimize them. But be assured that I would love to hear from you about the good and the bad, and to the best of my abilities, help you.

To echo the opening: I smile a little every time you pick up this book. I am grateful to have deserved a place in your attention and proud to have been given the opportunity. Thank you, and I love you.

*Maya Sozer*

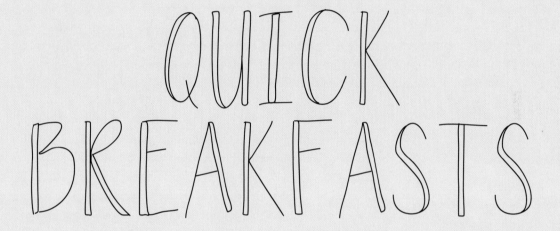

# QUICK BREAKFASTS

This one meal truly sets the tone for the rest of the day. I see breakfast as a quick, delicious and nutritious treat time. I want to start working already, but I also want to eat something that will make me start smiling and feeling good. Time being a prime asset in the morning, you need options. All of the recipes in this chapter are made to minimize your hands-on prep time. Some are thought of as quick put-together in the morning, with the possibility to take them on the go with you, if need be. Others are to be prepped the night before, so they are all ready to go in the morning. And yet some are for more relaxed mornings. They're all equally delicious.

# SAUTÉED MUSHROOM AND AVOCADO QUESADILLAS

gluten-free

I often default to quesadillas when I am out of time, out of other options or pretty much whenever I can create any other excuse to make them. Yes, the name *quesadilla* may imply cheese, but my version, as always, is vegan. No cheese is needed when you can use hummus. Trust me on this. Hummus, cooked in a sandwich, tastes absolutely fantastic, and it will even do a decent job at holding the sandwich together. For faster mornings, the sautéed mushroom used in this recipe can be made ahead of time and stored in the fridge.

## Serves 2

### SAUTÉED MUSHROOMS

2 tbsp (28 ml) olive oil

3 shallots, thinly sliced

Salt and freshly ground black pepper

6 medium portobello mushrooms, thinly sliced

### QUESADILLAS

4 tbsp (61 g) hummus

2 large tortillas

1 avocado, peeled, pitted and sliced

Fresh arugula

Heat the olive oil in a skillet over medium heat. Add the shallots and cook, stirring occasionally, until the shallots are translucent, about 3 minutes. Add salt and pepper to taste. Add the mushrooms and cook until most of the juice is reduced and the mushrooms turn golden brown. Spread 2 tablespoons (30 g) of the hummus over one side of a tortilla. Add half of the sautéed mushrooms over the hummus and fold the tortilla in half.

Cook both sides in a skillet until each side gets a nice crust with slightly charred spots (alternatively, cook in a panini maker). Repeat for the second quesadilla. After they are cooked, open the fold briefly to add the avocado slices and fresh arugula.

# ALMOND BUTTER BLUEBERRY PANCAKES

Life is so much better with pancakes, particularly the healthy and fluffy ones like these without a single hint of blandness. This has an exciting flavor profile with a little nuttiness and playfully embedded blueberries that not only add to the yumminess, but also work so well visually and texturally.

## Serves 2

### DRY INGREDIENTS
1 cup (125 g) all-purpose flour

2 tsp (5 g) ground cinnamon

1 tsp (5 g) baking powder

½ tsp baking soda

Pinch of salt

### WET INGREDIENTS
1 cup (235 ml) almond milk

1 tbsp (16 g) almond butter

2 tbsp (28 ml) maple syrup or agave nectar

1 tbsp (15 ml) pure vanilla extract

### TO COOK
Coconut oil, for coating the pan

¾ cup (37 g) fresh or frozen blueberries

### TO SERVE
Berries

Pure maple syrup

Mix the dry ingredients in a bowl and set aside.

Whisk the wet ingredients in a separate bowl, and combine with the dry ingredient mixture.

Heat some coconut oil in a pan over medium-low heat. When the oil is hot, add 2 tablespoons (28 ml) of the batter and add a few blueberries. Shape into a circle and cook each side for about 3 minutes, until you get a golden brown crust. Repeat with the rest of the batter.

Serve with additional berries and maple syrup, if desired.

# GREEN VELVET SMOOTHIE

gluten-free

This is not a brain-freeze cold smoothie. It is a comfort smoothie, especially suited for chillier mornings. And it is utterly smooth to the point of being velvety. You will see what I mean by that. If you are not used to kale smoothies, no need to worry. The taste is an absolute treat, and it is a perfect option for getting started with green smoothies.

## Serves 1

3 to 4 large kale leaves, stemmed

1 apple, cored

½ banana (can be frozen)

2 Medjool dates, pitted

1 tbsp (10 g) chia seeds

1 tbsp (16 g) peanut butter

1 cup (235 ml) cold almond milk

OPTIONAL TOPPINGS

Raspberries

Blueberries

Almond slices

Put all the ingredients in a high-speed blender and blend until smooth.

# QUICK PARFAIT

*gluten-free*

Yes, parfait still exists in the vegan world, and it can easily be made at home. Instead of yogurt, I am using a strawberry vanilla cashew cream, and if there is any difference, it is for the better. This thing is TASTY!

## Serves 2

1 cup (255 g) frozen strawberries

½ cup (70 g) raw cashews

¼ cup (60 ml) pure maple syrup

1 tsp (5 ml) pure vanilla extract

1 cup (100 g) vegan granola

Pomegranate seeds, for topping (optional)

Blend all the ingredients, except the granola and pomegranate seeds, in a high-speed blender until smooth. Assemble in cups by layering the cream and granola. Pomegranate seeds as decoration definitely adds to the look, texture and taste.

# SALTED TAHINI SPREAD

*gluten-free*

Peanut butter is great, but tahini is tahini! Try spreading this salted sweet tahini goodness over your bagel or toast in the morning. You can get creative and add chocolate, fruits or jelly.

Makes 1 cup (240 g) spread

½ cup (120 g) tahini

¼ cup (60 ml) pure maple syrup

1 tsp (5 ml) pure vanilla extract

¼ cup (60 ml) almond milk

½ tsp salt

Blend all the ingredients in a blender until smooth.

# DAY DREAM FRENCH TOAST

This vegan French toast is light and beautiful. This is a really good way to make use of the not-so-fresh-anymore bread—especially the firmer, artisan breads with a substantial crust, because those dry up way too quickly. For a faster start, you can make the batter ahead of time and keep it in the fridge overnight.

Serves 2

BATTER

1 cup (235 ml) almond milk

1 tsp (5 ml) pure vanilla extract

1 tbsp (15 ml) pure maple syrup

2 tbsp (8 g) arrowroot starch

1 tsp (3 g) ground cinnamon

¼ tsp ground nutmeg

1 tsp (5 ml) soy sauce

TO COOK

Coconut oil, for pan

4 slices day-old bagged vegan bread, sliced (firmer breads with a thick crust are better)

BERRY SAUCE (OPTIONAL)

1 cup (145 g) fresh or frozen berries

3 tbsp (45 ml) pure maple syrup

GARNISH (OPTIONAL)

Powdered sugar

Put the batter ingredients in a large bowl and mix thoroughly. Coat a pan with coconut oil and place over medium heat. When the pan is hot (but not smoking!), dip each slice of bread in the batter and cook on both sides until they are slightly browned. Meanwhile, cook the berry sauce ingredients in a saucepan over medium-low heat for about 2 minutes. Plate the toast, drizzle with the berry sauce and sprinkle with powdered sugar, if you like. If you didn't go for the berry sauce, you can just use the good old maple syrup.

# GOOD MORNING TIRAMISU

gluten-free

Sometimes there is a very good reason to wake up in the morning. And I love it when that reason is this tiramisu! This is not exactly the traditional tiramisu, rather, a lighter, portable version that is quickly prepared and served in a cup. There is no cooking or baking involved at all. Although it can be put together with little effort, this is thought of as a make-ahead recipe because it needs to stay in the fridge for a little while, preferably overnight. And that works perfectly for breakfast. Needless to say, it can be thoroughly enjoyed as a dessert anytime of the day.

Serves 3

### LEMON CUSTARD LAYER

¾ cup (105 g) raw cashews

¾ cup (175 ml) full-fat coconut milk

⅓ cup (80 ml) pure maple syrup

1 tbsp (15 ml) freshly squeezed lemon juice

Zest of ½ lemon

1 tsp (5 ml) pure vanilla extract

### COFFEE LAYER

1 cup (140 g) raw cashews

¼ cup (60 ml) almond milk

⅓ cup (80 ml) pure maple syrup

¼ cup (60 ml) brewed espresso, or 3 tsp (3 g) instant coffee mixed with ¼ cup (60 ml) hot water

3 tbsp (21 g) cacao powder

1 tbsp (15 ml) coconut oil, melted

1 tsp (5 ml) pure vanilla extract

### BETWEEN THE TWO LAYERS

1 cup (100 g) vegan granola or crumbled vegan cookies

In batches, blend the lemon custard layer ingredients and the coffee layer ingredients separately in a high-speed blender. No need to clean the blender in between. In a glass or a dessert cup, stack the two layer fillings and the granola in the arrangement you like. Keep in the refrigerator for at least 4 hours or overnight before serving.

# VANILLA SKY APPLE PIE SMOOTHIE

gluten-free

A frothy smoothie that feels like the best part of the fall season.

Serves 1 to 2

1 apple, cored

1 banana

1 cup (235 ml) almond milk

1 tbsp (16 g) peanut butter

1 tsp (5 ml) pure vanilla extract

¼ cup (20 g) rolled oats (certified gluten-free, if necessary)

Pinch of ground nutmeg (optional)

Apple slices for topping (optional)

1 tsp (2 g) ground cinnamon, plus more for garnish

Mix all the ingredients, except the extra cinnamon, in a high-speed blender. Transfer to a glass, optionally top with apple slices and sprinkle with ground cinnamon.

# PEANUT BUTTER BANANA PANCAKES

You already know and love pancakes; I don't need to convince anybody about how great they are for breakfast. But what I will claim is that a 100 percent whole wheat, vegan version is absolutely delicious and super easy to make from scratch.

Serves 2

### DRY INGREDIENTS

1 cup (130 g) whole wheat flour

2 tsp (5 g) ground cinnamon

1 tsp (5 g) baking powder

½ tsp baking soda

Pinch of salt

### WET INGREDIENTS

1 cup (235 ml) almond milk

1 banana

1 tbsp (16 g) peanut butter

2 tbsp (28 ml) pure maple syrup or agave nectar

1 tbsp (15 ml) pure vanilla extract

### TO COOK

Coconut oil, for pan

### OPTIONAL TOPPINGS

Coconut cream

Pure maple syrup

Strawberry halves

Mix the dry ingredients in a bowl and set aside. Whisk the wet ingredients together, making sure the peanut butter and banana fully blend in. Combine the dry and wet ingredients. Put some coconut oil in a skillet over medium-low heat and when the oil is hot enough, put in 2 tablespoons (28 ml) of the batter.

Shape into a circle and cook for about 2 minutes on each side, or until you are happy with the crust. Repeat with the rest of the batter.

Optionally top with coconut cream, maple syrup and strawberries.

# BANANA BREAD

This recipe is called a bread mostly due to the traditional naming. I view it as a cake, though. And I enjoy it as one. It is on the firmer side, lightly sweetened and moist but not mushy. The banana flavor is not overwhelming at all and the walnuts on top are an absolute treat.

Serves 4

1¼ cups (163 g) whole wheat flour

1 tsp (5 g) baking powder

½ tsp baking soda

Pinch of salt

2 ripe bananas

2 tbsp (28 ml) coconut oil, melted or olive oil (plus more for coating the pan)

½ cup (120 ml) pure maple syrup

1 tsp (5 ml) pure vanilla extract

1 tbsp (15 ml) dark rum (optional)

½ cup (60 g) roughly chopped walnuts

Oil, for pan

Preheat the oven to 350°F (175°C). Put all the dry ingredients, except the walnuts, in a bowl, mix and set aside. Put the bananas, coconut oil, maple syrup, vanilla and rum in a food processor and mix until puréed. Add the liquid and dry mixtures together and combine. Pour the batter into a lightly oiled 5 x 7-inch (13 x 18-cm) baking pan. Sprinkle the top of the batter with the walnuts. Bake for about 45 minutes. Keep an eye on it during baking and do the toothpick test (a toothpick inserted in the middle of the cake should come out clean) to judge when it is done.

# CHOCOLATE TAHINI GRANOLA

gluten-free

A good, healthy granola is a must-have because it is so super versatile: Good for just grabbing a handful and snacking on, eating as a cereal with a plant-based milk, adding to fruit salads, making parfaits or using in desserts are just some of the immediate uses that come to mind. This version has a fun twist or two, using tahini and coconut oil.

## Makes 4 cups (400 g) granola

¼ cup (60 ml) coconut oil, melted

¼ cup (60 g) tahini

¼ cup (60 ml) pure maple syrup or agave nectar

½ tsp salt

2 tbsp (14 g) cacao powder

1 tsp (2 g) ground cinnamon

3 cups (80 g) rolled oats (certified gluten-free, if necessary)

¼ cup (28 g) pecan pieces

SERVING SUGGESTIONS

Vegan yogurt

Almond milk

Cashew cream

Fresh berries

Preheat oven to 350°F (175°C). Mix the melted coconut oil, tahini, maple syrup, salt, cacao and cinnamon in a bowl, keeping the mixture warm and liquid. Add the oats and pecans and mix well. Spread the mixture evenly on a parchment paper–lined baking sheet and bake for 15 minutes. Stir with a spoon and bake for an additional 10 minutes. Let it cool and then store in an airtight container.

# MATCHA ALMOND SMOOTHIE

gluten-free

There are mornings when I wake up feeling like a turtle, just wanting to stay in my shell or move very slowly when I have to. This superfood matcha smoothie is the precise cure that helps boost me into the day. It is loaded with a ton of nutrients, antioxidants and a bit of caffeine: the way to start the day right. Matcha is a high-grade, powdered green tea that is grown in the shade. The stems and veins of the tea leaves are also removed, resulting in a smooth taste and a higher concentration of the good stuff. Matcha is an ancient tradition, and it is easy to tell why when you taste and experience it.

## Serves 1

1 banana, frozen

1 medium apple, cored

1 tbsp (16 g) almond butter

1 cup (235 ml) almond milk

¼ tsp matcha powder

2 Medjool dates, pitted

Various fresh fruits

Blend all the ingredients in a high-speed blender until smooth. Optionally serve with fresh fruits. Drink immediately.

# STRAWBERRY PARFAIT POPSICLE

*gluten-free*

A popsicle for breakfast may seem odd, but it's a favorite of mine—especially in the summer. This same recipe can be turned into overnight granola (fridge, instead of freezer), or the strawberry cream can be used in a parfait if you like your granola to crunch. Basically, pick your favorite texture, and rest assured that it will be delicious.

Makes 4 to 6 pops

STRAWBERRY CASHEW CREAM

1 cup (255 g) frozen strawberries

½ cup (70 g) raw cashews

½ cup (120 ml) full-fat coconut milk

⅓ cup (80 ml) pure maple syrup

1 tsp (5 ml) pure vanilla extract

Pinch of salt

1 cup (100 g) vegan chocolate granola

Melted vegan chocolate (optional)

Blend all the strawberry cashew cream ingredients in a high-speed blender until all smooth and creamy. Transfer to a bowl and mix in the granola. Fill the Popsicle molds using a spoon. Keep in the freezer overnight. Optionally dip in melted chocolate before eating.

# QUINOA PORRIDGE

*gluten-free*

A simple, warming, comforting porridge for when you need a little heat in your breakfast.

Serves 1 to 2

½ cup (87 g) uncooked quinoa

1 cup (235 ml) almond milk

2 tbsp (28 ml) coconut cream (optional)

½ tsp ground cinnamon

1½ tsp (8 ml) pure maple syrup (or more to taste)

1 tbsp (16 g) nut butter (optional)

OPTIONAL TOPPINGS

Fresh fruit

Candied pecans

Boil the quinoa in the almond milk and coconut cream (if using) until soft, about 15 minutes. Transfer to a bowl, add the cinnamon, maple syrup, nut butter and your favorite toppings. I love this topped with fresh fruits and/or candied pecans.

# BLUEBERRY CHIA OVERNIGHT OATS

gluten-free

Overnight oats are awesome, filling breakfast options that come with next to no effort. Just throw a few ingredients together, put it in the fridge and let time do all the work. You get to enjoy smooth, creamy and flavorful oats in the morning.

## Serves 1 to 2

½ cup (40 g) rolled oats (certified gluten-free, if necessary)

1 tbsp (10 g) chia seeds

½ cup (78 g) frozen or fresh blueberries

Juice of ½ lemon

1 cup (235 ml) almond milk

1½ tsp (8 ml) pure maple syrup or agave nectar

OPTIONAL TOPPINGS

Coconut Whipped Cream (page 156)

Blueberries

Combine all the ingredients, except the toppings, in a bowl. Cover and keep in the fridge overnight (it will actually keep in the fridge for a few days). I enjoyed mine served in a glass, topped with whipped coconut cream and blueberries.

# PINK PANTHER SMOOTHIE

gluten-free

There is something somewhat childish and ridiculously happy about having a pink smoothie. This one feels like a treat and passes as a meal or a nutritious snack.

## Serves 1

½ banana (optionally frozen)

⅓ cup (47 g) raw cashews

1 cup (255 g) frozen strawberries

½ cup (120 ml) almond milk (I use unsweetened)

1 tbsp (15 ml) pure maple syrup, or 2 Medjool dates

OPTIONAL TOPPINGS

Berries

Sliced almonds

Blend all the ingredients in a high-speed blender. Drink or enjoy as a smoothie bowl with toppings.

# CREAM OF SPINACH POCKETS

Spinach, cream and bread. There aren't many ways to go wrong, really. As easy as this is to prepare, the result is incredibly impressive, portable and satisfying. The filling itself can be prepped ahead and kept in the fridge for a quick grilled sandwich anytime.

Serves 2 to 3

CREAM SAUCE

¼ cup (60 ml) water

½ cup (70 g) raw cashews

3 tbsp (24 g) nutritional yeast

2 tbsp (28 ml) cider vinegar

Salt and freshly ground black pepper

FILLING

1 tbsp (15 ml) grapeseed or other vegetable oil

1 medium onion, chopped

2 cloves garlic, minced

1 cup (30 g) frozen spinach, thawed

¼ cup (15 g) chopped fresh parsley

4 medium pita pockets or tortillas

Vegan butter (optional)

Put all the cream sauce ingredients, including salt and pepper to taste, in a high-speed blender and mix until it is all smooth, then set aside.

To make the filling, heat the oil in a pan over medium heat and add the onion. Stir and cook for 3 to 5 minutes before adding the garlic and spinach. Cook them for an additional 3 minutes. Add the cashew cream sauce and cook until it thickens a little and has a creamy consistency, about 2 to 3 minutes. Turn off the heat and mix in the parsley.

Stuff each pita pocket with this filling or spread the filling over half of a tortilla and fold the other half over. Cook the filled pita or tortilla in a panini maker or a skillet. Optionally, spread vegan butter on the bread during cooking.

# HAZELNUT CHOCOLATE SPREAD

*gluten-free*

You know what this is and I believe you also have your own favorite way to have it for breakfast. May I suggest cooking it, such as in a grilled sandwich, or with a sesame seed bagel or even a tortilla? It is fun to just fantasize about this.

Makes 1 cup (260 g) spread

1 cup (135 g) roasted hazelnuts

¼ cup (60 ml) almond milk

3 tbsp (21 g) Dutch-processed cocoa powder

3 tbsp (45 ml) coconut oil

3 tbsp (45 ml) pure maple syrup

1 tsp (5 ml) pure vanilla extract

Pinch of salt

Chopped hazelnuts (optional)

Blend all the ingredients in a high-speed blender until smooth. Top with hazelnuts, if using. It can stay in the fridge for up to a week.

# CHOCOLATE SWIRL CAKE

If you are going to have tea for breakfast, you might as well make it an occasion and bake yourself a cake the day before. After all, breakfast sets the tone for the rest of the day and a chocolate swirl cake kind of day just sounds so great.

Serves 4

DRY INGREDIENTS

2 cups (250 g) all-purpose flour

1 tsp (5 g) baking powder

½ tsp baking soda

1 tsp (2 g) ground cinnamon

½ tsp ground nutmeg

Pinch of salt

1 tbsp (7 g) Dutch-processed cocoa powder

WET INGREDIENTS

2 bananas, mashed

¾ cup (175 ml) almond milk

¼ cup (60 ml) coconut oil

½ to ¾ cup (120 to 175 ml) pure maple syrup or agave nectar

2 tbsp (32 g) almond butter (or other nut butter)

1 tsp (5 ml) pure vanilla extract

Preheat the oven to 350°F (175°C). Mix all the dry ingredients, except the cocoa powder, in a large bowl and set aside. Mix all the wet ingredients in a separate bowl (you can use a blender for this). Combine the dry and wet mixtures together by folding with a spatula. Pour about two-thirds of the batter into a small baking pan (about 5 x 7 inches [13 x 18 cm]). Alternatively, you can use 4 muffin molds. Mix the cocoa powder into the remaining third of the batter and pour the chocolate batter over the white batter layer. Create marbling by swirling a fork once through both layers. Bake the cake for 45 to 50 minutes. The time may vary slightly depending on your oven. Check every now and then toward the end by dipping a toothpick in the center of the cake. It is done when the toothpick comes out clean. Remove the cake from the oven; let it cool for at least 1 hour before serving.

# BLUEBERRY CHIA SMOOTHIE

gluten-free

Chia seeds are just good for you. We all know that. But as nutritious as they are, their texture can be a challenge for some. Whether you are a chia seed fan or not, a refreshing and delicious smoothie is an easy, effective and delicious way to incorporate them into a nutrition bomb.

Serves 1

½ banana (optionally frozen)

2 kale leaves, stemmed

½ cup (78 g) frozen blueberries

½ cup (120 ml) almond milk (I use unsweetened)

1 tsp (5 ml) pure vanilla extract

1½ tsp (5 g) chia seeds

OPTIONAL

Strawberries, halved

Blackberries

Strawberry Cashew Cream (page 38)

Blend all the ingredients in a high-speed blender. This is better to drink while fresh, for the most benefit. I serve it with strawberry halves, blackberries and Strawberry Cashew Cream.

# EASY LUNCHES

Everyone has a favorite meal, and the one that I most look forward to is lunch. It is a good opportunity to take a midday break and let the imagination play a little, or if there are friends around, it is a great way to socialize. Either way, it deserves the time. The temptation to work through lunch, snack through it or just cram-something-down-your-throat-at-your-desk through it should be resisted.

The bar of expectations for a good lunch is quite high, however. First and foremost, it needs to be filling, and it needs to be fun, comforting, nourishing and energizing. Lunch is when the most food freedom should be allowed, both in variety and quantity. The best way to deliver on all these fronts is the home-cooked lunch. Here is the thing, though: It shouldn't take a lot of time to prepare, as it is better to spend the most time simply enjoying it.

# EGGPLANT QUINOA BLACK BEAN BURGER

*gluten-free*

A good way to infuse your vegan burgers with a smoky flavor is to use barbecued veggies, especially eggplant. I don't barbecue too often, but when I do, I like my beautifully grilled and slightly charred veggies to last a good part of the week. So, I grill quite a bit of them in one go. Another plus is that you can go creative with them and incorporate them in sauces, dips, panini, or as in this case, a burger patty. The recipe for the patty is below. I assembled my burger with vegan mayo, fresh baby spinach, sautéed mushrooms, pickled jalapeños, red onion and avocado (of course).

## Makes 4 patties

½ medium eggplant

½ medium red bell pepper

1 cup (100 g) cooked black beans

¾ cup (139 g) cooked quinoa

½ cup (60 g) vegan bread crumbs (gluten-free, if necessary)

½ red onion, finely chopped

1 tsp (3 g) ground cumin

1 tsp (3 g) chili powder

1 tsp (3 g) smoked paprika

Salt and freshly ground black pepper

Barbecue the eggplant and the red bell pepper with the skin on: Poke the eggplant a few times with a knife and place it, and the pepper, on a hot grill. Cook until the pepper skin is moderately charred. The eggplant, depending on size, may take longer and it will take the heat, so place it on the hottest spot and be patient until it gets all mushy. Alternatively, cut the eggplant in half lengthwise and also make a pattern of knife cuts on the flesh to aid in faster cooking, then roast the eggplant and the bell peppers at 450°F (230°C), for about 20 minutes, or until the eggplant is fully mushy and the pepper skins are moderately charred. When done, peel the skins off both and lower the oven to 400°F (200°C).

Put all the ingredients, including salt and black pepper to taste, in a large bowl. Mash and mix until it starts taking shape. Shape into 4 patties and cook in the oven for about 25 minutes.

# CURRIED VEGGIES

gluten-free

This is for anytime you need to feel warm, physically or emotionally. Spices do that. They add and amplify tastes and bring an almost three-dimensionality. You dive deeper into the taste with every bite until you feel all warmed up and engulfed by it. Spices are also known to be good for your health. For the uninitiated, spicy foods may be an acquired taste, and I wholeheartedly recommend acquiring it. This is a good start.

## Serves 3 to 4

2 tbsp (28 ml) coconut or olive oil

1 medium yellow onion, diced

2 to 3 cloves garlic, minced

1 tbsp (8 g) grated fresh ginger

1½ tbsp (10 g) curry powder

¼ tsp cayenne pepper

1 tbsp (16 g) tomato paste

VEGETABLES

1 cup (150 g) peas

2 medium potatoes

1 carrot, peeled and chopped

2 cups (200 g) cauliflower, broken into florets

½ jalapeño pepper, seeded and chopped

½ cup (90 g) coarsely chopped tomatoes

OR

5 cups (650 g) frozen mixed vegetables, thawed

2 cups (473 ml) vegetable stock or water

1 cup (235 ml) light or full-fat coconut milk

1 (15-oz [425-g]) can chickpeas, drained and rinsed

Sea salt and freshly ground black pepper

2 tbsp (28 ml) freshly squeezed lime juice

2 tbsp (2 g) chopped fresh cilantro

In a cast-iron skillet or a large pan, heat the oil over medium heat. Add the onion and cook, stirring occasionally, until the onion starts changing color. This should take 5 to 7 minutes. Add the garlic and ginger and cook, stirring, for another minute, to blend the flavors. Add the curry powder and cayenne and stir for 30 seconds to toast the spices. Add the tomato paste and stir until well blended, about 1 minute.

Add the vegetables, raise the heat to medium-high and stir for a minute, or until the veggies get warm. Add the veggie stock, coconut milk and chickpeas and bring to boil. Season to taste with salt and black pepper. Lower the heat to medium-low, cover and let simmer until the vegetables are tender, 20 to 25 minutes. Add the lime juice and cilantro and enjoy.

# MAKE IT YOURS CREAMY VEGGIE SOUP

gluten-free

This recipe will arm you with the delicious knowledge of "creamy" vegan soups. You can call yours broccoli and cheddar, cream of veggie, veggie chowder . . . you pick. The concept is the same and you can vary the vegetables used in here. You can also go for a frozen veggie mix for a faster recipe. All I know is that it will make you feel better in the way only a good soup can.

Serves 3

2 tbsp (28 ml) grapeseed or olive oil

1 onion, chopped

2 cloves garlic, minced

4 cups (946 ml) vegetable stock

Salt and freshly ground black pepper

VEGETABLES

1 medium carrot, chopped

2 cups (200 g) broccoli florets, chopped

1 stalk celery, chopped

OR

3 cups (390 g) frozen mixed vegetables, thawed

CREAM

1 cup (140 g) raw cashews

3 tbsp (24 g) nutritional yeast

1 tsp (3 g) garlic powder

Heat the oil in a medium pot over medium heat, then add the onion and garlic. Cook, stirring, for 5 minutes, or until the onion changes color. Add the veggies and cook for a minute (cook for a little longer if using frozen veggies). Add the vegetable stock, stir and bring to boil. Add salt and pepper to taste, lower the heat to medium-low and simmer until the vegetables are tender, 20 to 25 minutes.

In the meantime, blend all the cream ingredients, plus 1 cup (235 ml) of water, in a high-speed blender. When the veggies are done, slowly add the cream mixture while stirring. Alternatively (if you don't want any texture but prefer a silky smooth soup), you can leave the blended cream mixture in the blender, add the cooked vegetable mixture and blend again. Adjust for salt and let cook for another 3 to 5 minutes.

# BETTER NOT SQUASH MAC & CHEESE

What if mac & cheese was all vegan and spicy, too, for even more heat? I know mac & cheese is a classic, but it is still a lot of fun to play with the concept. This works for me on so many levels.

Serves 3

¼ cup (35 g) raw cashews

1¾ cups (315 g) cooked butternut squash, or ¾ (15-oz [425-g]) can

2 tbsp (28 ml) olive oil

1¾ cups (414 ml) almond milk

¼ cup (32 g) nutritional yeast

1 tbsp (15 ml) freshly squeezed lemon juice

2 tsp (4 g) sweet curry powder

1 to 2 tsp (3 to 6 g) grated fresh ginger

1 tsp (4 g) Mustard (page 175) or Dijon mustard

2 tsp (6 g) garlic powder

2 tsp (5 g) onion powder

¼ tsp ground nutmeg

⅛ tsp cayenne pepper

Salt and freshly ground black pepper

1 lb (455 g) pasta

OPTIONAL GARNISH

Fresh thyme

Hemp seeds

Put all the ingredients, except the salt, black pepper and pasta, in a food processor and mix until smooth. Add salt and black pepper to taste.

Cook the pasta according to the package instructions. Add the butternut squash sauce to the same pot after draining out the pasta water. Cook, stirring, over medium-high heat for 3 to 4 minutes, or until the macaroni is uniformly dressed with the sauce and the sauce is hot.

# CURRIED CHICKPEA TACOS

*gluten-free*

Let's make a little unusual taco, with curried chickpeas for the spicy protein element together with an awesome, perfectly complementing red cabbage and avocado salad. Because we know that anything in a tortilla shell is allowed to be tacos and that tacos won't judge. Both the chickpeas and the red cabbage salad can be made ahead, to be assembled into tacos at lunchtime.

## Serves 2

### CURRIED CHICKPEAS

1 (15-oz [425-g]) can chickpeas, drained and rinsed

1½ tsp (3 g) curry powder

1 tsp (3 g) garlic powder

1 tbsp (15 ml) olive oil

1 tsp (5 ml) hot sauce

### RED CABBAGE SALAD

2 cups (140 g) shaved red cabbage (shave with a peeler)

½ cup (35 g) chopped lettuce

1 tbsp (15 ml) olive oil

Juice of ½ lemon

1 radish, sliced

1 cucumber, cubed

6 cherry tomatoes, cut in half

1 avocado, peeled, pitted and cubed

Salt

4 soft tortillas (I used wheat)

Place all the ingredients for the curried chickpeas in a pan over medium-high heat and cook for 5 to 7 minutes. Mix the salad ingredients in a large bowl. Heat the tortillas in a panini maker, in a pan or directly over the stovetop until you get a little charring and crispness. Stuff the tortillas with the fillings.

# COZY QUINOA LENTIL MINESTRONE

gluten-free

Everyone's definition of comfort food differs, and you don't have to pick just one. But if I had to pick, it would look like this: hearty and hot and nourishing. Enjoy it alongside some rice for an extra kick of comfort.

Serves 2 to 3

3 tbsp (45 ml) olive oil

2 cups (140 g) chopped mushrooms

1 onion, chopped

2 to 3 cloves garlic, minced

½ cup (96 g) dried green lentils

¼ cup (43 g) uncooked quinoa

2½ cups (590 ml) vegetable stock or water

½ tsp dried thyme

¼ tsp cayenne pepper

1 bay leaf

Salt

¼ cup (60 ml) coconut cream

¼ cup (32 g) nutritional yeast

3 handfuls of baby spinach

Heat 1 tablespoon (15 ml) of the olive oil in a skillet over medium heat. Add the mushrooms, stir and cook until the mushrooms lose their water and turn golden brown. Set aside. Add the remaining 2 tablespoons (28 ml) of the olive oil in a separate pot or saucepan with a lid, add the onion and garlic and cook for 3 to 5 minutes over medium heat, until the onion turns translucent. Rinse the lentils and quinoa and add them to the pot along with the vegetable stock, thyme, cayenne and bay leaf. Stir, add salt to taste and bring to a boil. Lower the heat and cook for about 20 minutes with the lid on.

Finally, add the coconut cream, nutritional yeast, baby spinach and cooked mushrooms. Adjust the salt and cook for another 3 minutes.

# CAST-IRON BLACK BEAN LOAF

gluten-free

This ridiculously filling lunch has an impressive taste and a lot of protein. It is very easy to put together but it takes a bit of oven time, so it is better to prep this the night before. It will rock your lunch the next day.

Serves 3

2 tbsp (28 ml) olive or grapeseed oil

1 medium onion, chopped

1 to 2 cloves garlic, minced

1 carrot, chopped

1 stalk celery, sliced

2 tbsp (28 ml) tamari

2 tbsp (32 g) tomato paste

½ tsp dried thyme

1 tbsp (8 g) arrowroot starch or cornstarch

1 cup (185 g) cooked quinoa

1 (15-oz [425-g]) can black beans, drained and rinsed

SAUCE

¼ cup (60 g) ketchup

2 tbsp (28 ml) pure maple syrup or agave nectar

Preheat the oven to 350°F (175°C). Heat the oil in a cast-iron pan over medium heat and add the onion. Cook, stirring, for 5 minutes. Add all the rest of the ingredients, except the sauce ingredients, and cook, stirring, for another minute. Transfer to the oven and bake for 30 minutes. Mix together the sauce ingredients in a small bowl and spread over the black bean loaf. Bake for another 30 minutes.

# FETTUCCINE ALFREDO

A no-compromise, easy vegan interpretation of the classic fettuccine Alfredo that just works. If you are a pasta lover like me, you will be one very happy luncher.

Serves 2 to 3

8 to 10 oz (225 to 280 g) fettuccine pasta

SAUCE

½ cup (70 g) raw cashews

¼ cup (32 g) nutritional yeast

1 tbsp (15 ml) olive oil

2 tsp (6 g) garlic powder

1½ cups (355 ml) almond milk

Juice and zest of ½ lemon

Salt and freshly ground black pepper

VEGETABLES

2 tbsp (28 ml) olive oil

2 cups (140 g) chopped mushrooms

¾ cup (113 g) peas

OPTIONAL GARNISH

Chopped green onions

Chopped parsley

Red pepper flakes

Cook the pasta according to the package instructions. Blend the sauce ingredients, including salt and pepper to taste, in a high-speed blender until smooth. To cook the vegetables, heat the olive oil in a skillet over medium heat and add the mushrooms. Cook, stirring until the mushrooms lose their water and turn golden brown, about 5 to 7 minutes. Add the peas and cook for another minute. Add the sauce, stir and cook for 3 more minutes. Combine the vegetable mixture with the cooked pasta and mix well. Serve warm.

# LENTIL BALLS

Lentil balls are one of my favorite—or probably the favorite—originally vegan, traditional Turkish foods. They are enjoyed and cherished regularly in pretty much every Turkish household. One interesting fact is that they did not emerge as meat imitations, but earned their place in that vast cuisine completely on their own merits. I keep repeating that lentils are magical because they pack jaw-dropping amounts of protein and fiber (around 15 grams of each in ¼ cup [50 g]!).

The recipe calls for fine bulgur, which can be found in all Middle Eastern markets. While you may find bulgur more easily in health food stores, those are usually not finely grained enough.

Here are some insider tips: Enjoy these cold or at room temperature. They can wait in the fridge for the next day, too.

Serves 2 to 3

1 cup (192 g) dried red lentils

Salt

½ cup (115 g) fine bulgur

¼ cup (60 ml) olive oil

1 medium onion, finely chopped

1 tsp (3 g) ground cumin

½ tsp dried mint (optional)

¼ tsp red pepper flakes

2 tbsp (32 g) tomato paste

1 tsp (2 g) ground sumac (optional)

¼ tsp freshly ground black pepper

1 cup (60 g) chopped parsley

6 green onions, chopped

3 lettuce leaves, sliced

Juice of 1 lemon

FOR SERVING

Whole lettuce leaves

Freshly squeezed lemon juice

Red pepper flakes

Rinse the lentils, then boil them in 3 cups (710 ml) of water, together with some salt, until they are fully soft and mushy. Turn off the heat and add the bulgur. Stir, cover and set aside to cool. Heat the olive oil on medium-high heat in a skillet and add the onion. Cook for 2 minutes. Add the cumin, dried mint (if using) and red pepper flakes. Cook for another minute. Add the tomato paste and cook for an additional 2 minutes. Combine with the lentil and bulgur mixture. Stir in the rest of the spices, plus salt to taste. Remove from the heat. When the mixture is near room temperature (to make sure it doesn't cook the greens), add the parsley, green onions, sliced lettuce and lemon juice. Shape into balls, and enjoy at room temperature or cold. Serve with a lot of fresh lettuce leaves and lemon. Wrap in the leaves, squeeze on a little lemon juice, sprinkle with some extra red pepper flakes and ride the wave of utter deliciousness.

# SPROUTED GREEN LENTIL PATTIES

gluten-free

This patty is a big-time winner with a delicious texture. Green lentils pack a lot in their cute, tiny shapes. They are protein and fiber powerhouses and somehow they get even better when sprouted. Just soak them in water for two days and change their water daily. There is bit of a wait—this recipe needs to be planned ahead—but the actual effort is very minimal and the result is impressive. These can function as burger patties or as a stand-alone protein.

## Serves 2 to 3

½ cup (96 g) dried green lentils

1 onion, chopped

1 medium carrot, chopped

¼ cup (15 g) chopped fresh parsley

2 tbsp (32 g) tomato paste

2 cloves garlic

2 tsp (5 g) ground cumin

1 tbsp (15 ml) olive oil

Pinch of cayenne pepper

Salt and freshly ground black pepper

¼ cup (28 g) finely chopped pecans or walnuts (optional)

Sprout the lentils for 2 days by soaking them in a bowl of water, changing the water daily. When they are sprouted, drain the water and rinse the lentils. Put all the ingredients, except the nuts, and including salt and black pepper to taste, in a food processor and grind until you have a uniform but still grainy texture. Mix in the nuts (if using) and shape the mixture into 4 patties. Panfry both sides until you get a golden crust, about 3 to 4 minutes each side, or bake in a preheated 400°F (200°F) oven for 25 to 30 minutes, or until they develop a golden brown crust.

# TOFU TASTE CUBES

Here is one easy way to make a warming, spicy and tasty tofu dish that goes well by itself or in a sandwich (I am also thinking tacos!). While the sauce ingredients are kept limited to a simple set, feel free to experiment with your favorite spices. Tofu will appreciate it. I love to serve it on a bagel (pictured).

Serves 1 to 2

SAUCE

2 tbsp (32 g) tomato paste

2 tbsp (28 ml) soy sauce

1 tsp (1 g) red pepper flakes

½ tsp ground cumin

½ tsp garlic powder

Salt and freshly ground black pepper

THE REST

2 tbsp (28 ml) grapeseed oil or other vegetable oil

1 carrot, diced

1 stalk celery, diced

8 oz (225 g) extra-firm tofu, diced

¼ cup (32 g) nutritional yeast

In a bowl, mix together all the sauce ingredients, including salt and black pepper to taste, plus ¼ cup (60 ml) of water. Heat the oil in a pan over medium heat. Add the carrot and celery and cook for 1 minute. Add the tofu and the sauce and cook, stirring, for 5 to 7 minutes. Adjust the salt. Turn off the heat, add the nutritional yeast and mix.

# SUSHI BOWL

*gluten-free*

I am all for cheating and enjoying the sushi taste with minimal effort. Recreating the sushi taste in a bowl also makes it easy to tote around as lunch.

Serves 2 to 3

1 cup (195 g) uncooked short-grain rice (white or brown)

1 (8 x 8-inch [20 x 20-cm]) sheet dried nori, or 1 (0.4-oz [11.3-g]) package wasabi roasted seaweed

1 carrot, chopped or spiraled

1 avocado, peeled, pitted and sliced

1 small cucumber, chopped or spiraled

2 small radishes, sliced

TOPPINGS

Sesame seeds (black and/or white)

Pickled ginger slices

SAUCE

2 tbsp (28 ml) tamari (for gluten-free) or soy sauce

3 tbsp (45 ml) rice vinegar

1½ tsp (8 ml) pure maple syrup or agave nectar

Boil or steam the rice according to the package instructions. Slice the nori sheet into strips and mix with the rice in a bowl. Add the vegetables and toppings. Mix the sauce ingredients separately and serve alongside.

# CAULIFLOWER RICE STIR-FRY

*gluten-free*

This is not rice with cauliflower. This is cauliflower used as rice and it is good for a number of reasons besides being really delicious. As much as I love rice, I like alternatives so I can moderate the quantity of starch I consume. This recipe offers a less starchy, less calorie-dense and more nutrient-rich option. I also like using this, without the seasoning, as a plain white rice side to other dishes.

## Serves 2 to 3

1 medium cauliflower

2 tbsp (28 ml) grapeseed oil

1 cup (130 g) frozen peas

½ cup (65 g) frozen corn

SEASONING

½ cup (120 ml) tamari (for gluten-free) or soy sauce

2 tbsp (28 ml) rice vinegar

1 clove garlic, minced

1 tsp (5 ml) pure maple syrup or agave nectar

2 tsp (2 g) minced fresh ginger

1 tsp (3 g) arrowroot starch

1 tsp (5 ml) hot sauce

OPTIONAL GARNISHES

Black sesame seeds

Watermelon radish slices

Lime slices

Spinach

Separate the cauliflower florets and discard the core. In a food processor, working in several batches, pulse the florets into roughly the size of a cooked rice grain. Heat the grapeseed oil in a skillet over medium-high heat. Cook the peas and corn for about a minute. Add the seasoning ingredients and cook, stirring, for 3 to 5 more minutes. Finally, add the cauliflower rice and stir-fry for 1 to 2 minutes. Garnish as desired.

# BLACK RICE PEAS

*gluten-free*

This looks really pretty in person. AND the looks are well supported by the taste, texture and nutrition.

Serves 2 to 3

1 cup (185 g) uncooked black rice

2 tbsp (28 ml) olive oil

1 medium red onion, chopped

2 cloves garlic

2 cups (260 g) fresh or frozen peas (thawed if frozen)

¼ cup (32 g) nutritional yeast

2 tbsp (7 g) chopped sun-dried tomatoes

2 tbsp (12 g) fresh mint leaves, sliced

Boil the rice in 4 cups (946 ml) of water until the rice softens. Note that this will not get as soft as white rice; it will stay firm. Drain the rice and transfer it to a large bowl. Heat the olive oil in a skillet over medium-high heat. Add the onion and cook for 5 minutes, stirring occasionally. Add the garlic and peas and cook until peas are done, about 10 minutes. Turn off the heat and mix in the nutritional yeast. Add the pea mixture to the rice, together with the sun-dried tomatoes and mint leaves, and mix. Serve warm or cold.

# COCONUT CURRY POLENTA WITH SAUTÉED MUSHROOMS

*gluten-free*

This turned me into a polenta lover. It totally felt like a big, warm hug and a pat on the back. Pairing this with sautéed mushrooms is the cherry on top.

Serves 3 to 4

### SAUTÉED MUSHROOMS

2 tbsp (28 ml) olive oil

1 medium onion, chopped

2 cloves garlic, minced

3 cups (210 g) sliced mixed or button mushrooms

1 tbsp (15 ml) freshly squeezed lemon juice

Salt and freshly ground black pepper

### CURRIED POLENTA

18 oz (510 g) precooked polenta

¼ cup (60 ml) coconut cream

2 tsp (6 g) finely grated fresh ginger

1 tsp (5 g) sweet curry

½ tsp garlic powder

½ tsp ground cumin

¼ tsp cayenne pepper

2 tbsp (28 ml) olive oil

To sauté the mushrooms, heat the olive oil in skillet over medium-high heat. When the oil is hot but not smoking, add the onion and cook, stirring, for 5 minutes. Add the garlic, mushrooms, lemon juice, and salt and black pepper to taste. Cook, stirring, until the mushrooms lose their water and turn golden brown.

Mix together all the curried polenta ingredients, except the olive oil, in a large bowl and set aside. Heat the olive oil in skillet over medium-high heat, add the polenta mixture and cook for 7 to 10 minutes. Serve the mushrooms over a bed of curried polenta.

# GREEN LENTIL BURGERS

This recipe is more in the Mediterranean tradition, really. With this one, you won't find that sweet, mushy blob that is often passed off as a vegan patty. This is the real deal.

## Serves 2 to 3

1 cup (192 g) uncooked green lentils

Salt

1 medium onion, chopped

2 cloves garlic, minced

½ cup (60 g) vegan bread crumbs

3 tbsp (24 g) nutritional yeast

Juice and zest of ½ lemon

1 tsp (3 g) ground cumin

½ tsp freshly ground black pepper

Grapeseed or other high-heat vegetable oil (optional)

SUGGESTED GARNISHES

Cherry tomatoes

Vegan mayonnaise (page 179)

Pickled jalapeños

Lettuce

Kale Mint Pesto (page 163)

Buns

The key thing about this recipe is not to cook lentils for too long. We don't want them too soft. Put the lentils in a pot with 3 cups (710 ml) of cold water, add some salt and cook over medium heat for about 10 minutes. The lentils should become just about soft enough to eat. Drain the lentils and put them in a food processor together with all the other ingredients, including salt to taste. Mix them carefully, leaving a chunky texture. Taste and adjust for salt. Form the mixture into patties and bake in a preheated 400°F (200°C) oven for 15 minutes. For a crispier texture, you can pan-fry on both sides in a pan lightly coated with a high-temperature oil until you are happy with the crusting. Garnish with cherry tomatoes, mayo, pickled jalapeños, lettuce, pesto and on a bun, if you wish.

# QUINOA WALNUT BURGERS

This comes with a lot of protein, fiber and an overall feeling of well-being. I love the texture of walnuts in here and it has a mouthful of delicious flavor. As with other burger patty recipes in this book, these can be stored frozen after cooking, ready to be turned into a burger whenever the need or the craving arises.

Makes 3 to 4 patties

⅓ cup (58 g) uncooked quinoa

⅓ cup (64 g) dried green lentils

1 medium onion, chopped

1 clove garlic

3 tbsp (24 g) nutritional yeast

1 tsp (3 g) ground cumin

1 tsp (2 g) freshly ground black pepper

½ cup (60 g) vegan bread crumbs

Salt

¼ cup (30 g) chopped walnuts

Grapeseed or other high-heat vegetable oil, for pan (optional)

OPTIONAL GARNISH

Whole wheat bun

Sliced avocado

Sautéed mushrooms (page 14)

Vegan mayonnaise (page 179)

Cranberries

Sprouts

Rinse the quinoa and the lentils, then boil in 3 cups (710 ml) of water until they are cooked but still retain a firm texture, about 10 minutes. Drain the cooked lentils and quinoa and place in a food processor. Add the rest of the ingredients, except the walnuts and oil, and including salt to taste, and mix. Add the walnuts and pulse a few times. Shape the mixture into patties and cook for 3 to 4 minutes on each side in a skillet coated with oil. Alternatively, you can bake the patties in a preheated 400°F (200°C) oven for 20 to 25 minutes. I assemble my burger in a whole wheat bun with avocado slices, sautéed mushrooms, vegan mayo, cranberries and sprouts.

# SAUCY RICE STIR-FRY

*gluten-free*

This hearty veggie rice stir-fry has a deeply yummy and bold sauce—all I really need from a satisfying lunch. I know that no excuse is ever necessary to make rice stir-fries, but this also happens to be a good way to use yesterday's leftover rice. It is actually better with the day-old rice.

## Serves 2

### SAUCE

½ cup (120 ml) tamari (for gluten-free) or soy sauce

½ cup (120 ml) vegetable stock

2 tbsp (28 ml) rice vinegar

1 clove garlic, minced

1 tsp (5 ml) pure maple syrup or agave nectar

1½ tsp (4 g) grated fresh ginger

1 tbsp (8 g) arrowroot starch

½ tsp red pepper flakes

### STIR-FRY

2 tbsp (28 ml) grapeseed oil

6 oz (170 g) mixed shiitake and portobello mushrooms

1 cup (71 g) broccoli florets

½ cup (65 g) frozen peas

2 cups (256 g) cooked rice

3 to 4 green onions

Mix together the sauce ingredients in a bowl and set aside. Heat the grapeseed oil in a stir-fry pan over medium-high heat. Add the vegetables, except the green onions, and cook, stirring, for 5 minutes. Add the sauce and cook for about 2 more minutes, or until the sauce starts to thicken. Add the rice and green onions and stir-fry for a minute.

# SPICY POTATO LEEK SALAD

*gluten-free*

Potatoes and leeks play so well together, and they love their spices. This is named as a salad but it will be just as happy snuggled inside a sandwich, a savory pastry or a collard wrap, to name a few. Try this as a bruschetta over roasted eggplant slices!

## Serves 2

4 medium potatoes, skin on

2 tbsp (28 ml) olive oil

1 cup (130 g) frozen peas, thawed

1 leek, thinly sliced

2 to 3 cloves garlic, minced

1 tsp (3 g) grated fresh ginger

1 tsp (3 g) ground cumin

½ tsp garam masala

Salt and freshly ground black pepper

1 tbsp (15 ml) freshly squeezed lemon juice

¼ cup (4 g) fresh cilantro, chopped

Wash and cube the potatoes and boil until they are soft, about 20 minutes. Mash them with a fork and set aside. Heat the olive oil in a pan over medium heat. Add the peas, leek, garlic, ginger, cumin, garam masala and salt and pepper to taste. Cook, stirring, for about 3 minutes. Add the mashed potatoes, stir and continue to cook for another 2 minutes.

Turn off the heat and add the lemon juice and cilantro.

# SPICY RED LENTIL SOUP

gluten-free

It turns out that vegan soups are really, really hard to come by in non-vegan restaurants. It is either chicken noodle or cream of something. That's where this Turkish-inspired red lentil soup comes in. On top of the classic recipe, I added a few spices and items that I think gives the flavor an edge. The result was an absolute hit. Protein, veggies and spices are all covered.

Other ideas to try to add to this soup: lemon zest, saffron, dried mint leaves. Basically, it is a good base soup to play with. If you love it, it rewards you. By the way, I must point out that the bay leaf is a must addition, in my opinion, for its wonderful fragrance.

Serves 2 to 3

### SOUP

1 onion, chopped

1 clove garlic, crushed

2 tbsp (28 ml) olive oil

1 carrot, chopped

1 stalk celery, chopped

1 medium potato, chopped

½ cup (90 g) diced tomato

½ tsp ground cumin

¼ tsp ground coriander

¼ tsp freshly ground black pepper

⅛ tsp ground turmeric

¾ cup (144 g) dried red lentils

1 bay leaf

Salt

Juice of ½ lemon

### GARNISHES

Freshly squeezed lemon juice

Fresh mint leaves

Red pepper flakes

Olive oil

In a large pot, sauté the onion and garlic in olive oil over medium-high heat until they change color, about 3 minutes. Add the rest of the vegetables and the spices and continue to cook for another 2 minutes. Add 4 cups (946 ml) of water and the lentils and bay leaf. Add salt to taste. Bring to a boil and lower the heat to low. Simmer until the lentils are soft, about 20 minutes (depending on the kind of lentils). Turn off the heat and purée with an immersion blender, if desired. Mix in the lemon juice. Pour in to soup bowls and add the garnishes.

# ZUCCHINI FRITTERS

This has a big flavor you wouldn't normally associate with zucchini. It definitely is a comfort food, right up there with potato fries or hash maybe. The difference is that this one is superhealthy, packed with fiber and nutrition. It is also easy and versatile. It will stay in the fridge and can be enjoyed hot or cold, as a stand-alone meal, as a side or even in sandwiches. You don't have to restrict it to just lunch, either.

Serves 2 to 3

3 medium zucchini

Salt and freshly ground black pepper

¼ cup (16 g) fresh parsley, chopped

¼ cup (15 g) fresh dill, chopped

4 green onions, chopped

1 clove garlic, minced

Zest of ½ lemon

2 tbsp (24 g) hemp seeds (optional)

½ cup (65 g) whole wheat flour

2 tbsp (16 g) cornstarch

1 tsp (5 g) baking powder

2 tbsp (28 ml) olive oil

Grate the zucchini into a bowl, toss with salt and wait for 10 minutes. Squeeze the zucchini with your hands to get the excess liquid out and place in a dry bowl. Add the herbs, onion, garlic, lemon zest and hemp seeds.

In a small bowl, mix the flour, cornstarch and baking powder with salt and pepper to taste (there is already salt in the zucchini, so don't add a lot here). Combine with the zucchini mixture. In a pan, heat the olive oil over medium-low heat. Put 2 tablespoons (28 ml) of the zucchini batter in the pan and spread into a circle. Make sure it is not too thick, so that it can cook thoroughly. Cook on both sides for about 3 minutes per side and continue until all the batter is cooked.

# TAKEAWAY SANDWICH

This is one complete and delicious sandwich filling that can stay in the fridge, ready to be dropped between two slices of bread at a moment's notice. It hits so many different spots with a rich and well-balanced flavor, texture and nutrition. It's a personal favorite.

Serves 3

1 (15-oz [425-g]) can chickpeas, drained and rinsed

2 medium potatoes, boiled and chopped

1 stalk celery, finely chopped

¼ red onion, finely chopped (optional)

½ cup (55 g) pecans, coarsely chopped

½ cup (60 g) dried cranberries

½ cup (115 g) vegan mayonnaise (page 179)

2 tbsp (16 g) nutritional yeast

2 tbsp (30 ml) freshly squeezed lemon juice

½ tsp garlic powder

2 cups (135 g) chopped kale

Salt and freshly ground black pepper

Poppy seed bun (optional)

Sprouts (optional)

Pulse the chickpeas in a food processor (or use a potato masher) and combine with all the other ingredients, including salt and black pepper to taste, in a bowl. Cover and keep in the fridge. I serve mine in a poppy seed bun, garnished with sprouts.

# TOFU ÉTOUFFÉE

gluten-free

When properly seasoned, tofu totally transforms from bland to glorious. One of the best ways to effectively infuse flavor into tofu is to crumble it, greatly increasing its surface area and giving the seasoning more places to hang on to. This filling protein bomb is all about a rich flavor and an intense, comforting heat.

Serves 2 to 3

16 oz (455 g) extra-firm tofu

2 tbsp (28 ml) olive oil

1 medium onion, diced

1 stalk celery, finely chopped

1 green bell pepper, seeded and finely diced

2 tsp (5 g) ground cumin

1 tsp (2 g) cayenne pepper

1 tsp (2 g) freshly ground black pepper

1 tsp (3 g) paprika

1 tsp (1 g) dried thyme

1 tbsp (16 g) tomato paste

½ cup (120 ml) coconut milk

1 bay leaf

Salt

OPTIONAL TOPPINGS

Parsley

Green onions

Rice

Crumble the tofu by hand into irregularly sized pieces. Heat the olive oil in a pan over medium heat. Sauté the onion, celery and bell pepper for 7 to 10 minutes. Add the tofu and spices and cook for another minute. Add the tomato paste, coconut milk, ½ cup (120 ml) of water and the bay leaf. Add salt to taste and cook, stirring, for 3 more minutes. Turn off the heat and garnish with chopped parsley and green onions. Serve it on rice.

# KALE SALAD WITH CURRY DRESSING

*gluten-free*

This one's for those who like their salads filling, spicy and interesting. And we also have to do the customary acknowledgment of the protein here, thanks to the superfood duo of quinoa and lentils.

## Serves 1 to 2

### SALAD

¼ cup (43 g) uncooked quinoa

¼ cup (48 g) dried green lentils

5 kale leaves, stemmed and chopped

½ cup (90 g) chopped tomato

¼ cup (35 g) chopped cucumber

¼ red onion, chopped

### CURRY TAHINI DRESSING

⅓ cup (80 g) tahini

Juice of 1 lemon

2 tbsp (28 ml) tamari

2 tbsp (4 g) curry powder

Freshly ground black pepper

Rinse the quinoa and lentils and place in a pot along with 2½ cups (590 ml) of water. Boil until soft, about 25 minutes. Drain and toss together with the rest of the salad ingredients. Combine the dressing ingredients and ¼ cup (60 ml) of water in a small bowl. Drizzle over the salad.

# CHANA MASALA

gluten-free

This is one of my favorite dishes, particularly on cold days. You know those days when you crave and need a hot meal to feel okay; this will hit the spot. Incorporating a healthy protein element using chickpeas and typically served with (or over) rice, it is a balanced meal that leaves you satisfied. I must warn you, though, a love for spices is a prerequisite to appreciating this recipe.

Serves 2 to 3

2 tbsp (28 ml) olive oil

1 medium onion, chopped

½ cup (125 g) tomato puree

2 cloves garlic, minced

1 tbsp (8 g) grated fresh ginger

1 tbsp (7 g) ground cumin

1 tbsp (7 g) garam masala

2 tsp (4 g) ground coriander

1 tsp (15 ml) freshly squeezed lemon juice

1 tsp (2 g) freshly ground black pepper

1 tsp (3 g) dry mustard

1 tsp (6 g) fine-grain sea salt

½ tsp ground turmeric

½ tsp chili powder

¼ tsp cayenne pepper

1 tbsp (1 g) chopped fresh cilantro (optional)

1 bay leaf (optional)

1 (15-oz [425-g]) can chickpeas, drained and rinsed

TO SERVE (OPTIONAL)

Cooked rice (basmati or your favorite)

Chopped fresh cilantro

Heat the olive oil in a saucepan over medium heat. Add the onion and cook until the onion starts changing color, about 5 minutes. Add the tomato puree and garlic and stir a few times. Add the rest of the ingredients, except the bay leaf and chickpeas. Continue to cook, stirring, for a few more minutes, then add ½ cup (120 ml) of water and the bay leaf. Add the chickpeas and cook, stirring, for 2 more minutes. Enjoy while hot. I recommend serving with rice. You can also garnish with chopped cilantro, if desired.

# KUNG PAO CHICKPEAS

gluten-free

It turns out, chickpeas do belong in a Kung Pao sauce, which has a delightful balance of sweet and sour. If you prefer, you can use a store-bought version of the sauce to save time.

Serves 2 to 3

### MARINATED CHICKPEAS

1 (15-oz [425-g]) can chickpeas, drained and rinsed

1 tbsp (15 ml) tamari (for gluten-free) or soy sauce

2 tbsp (28 ml) rice vinegar

1 tbsp (15 ml) pure maple syrup or agave nectar

1 tbsp (8 g) arrowroot starch or cornstarch

### SAUCE

2 tbsp (28 ml) balsamic vinegar

2 tbsp (28 ml) tamari (for gluten-free) or soy sauce

1 tsp (5 ml) hoisin sauce

1 tsp (5 ml) sesame oil

1 tsp (3 g) arrowroot starch or cornstarch

1 tsp (5 ml) pure maple syrup or agave nectar

### TO STIR-FRY

2 tbsp (28 ml) grapeseed oil or other high-heat vegetable oil

¼ cup (35 g) dry-roasted peanuts

2 cloves garlic, minced

1 tsp (3 g) grated fresh ginger

1 tbsp (15 ml) hot sauce or (15 g) red pepper flakes

1 bell pepper, seeded and chopped

3 green onions, coarsely sliced

### TO SERVE (OPTIONAL)

Chopped cilantro

Cooked rice

Mix the marinated chickpeas ingredients in a large bowl and set aside while you prepare the rest of the ingredients. In a separate bowl, mix together the sauce ingredients and set aside. Heat the grapeseed oil in a stir-fry pan over medium-high heat. Add the chickpea mixture and the peanuts and cook for 5 to 7 minutes, then add the garlic, ginger and hot sauce. Cook for another 2 minutes, then add the bell pepper, green onions and the sauce mixture. Cook briefly, stirring, for about 30 seconds. Garnish with the cilantro and serve with cooked rice.

# UDON NOODLES

I have met people who don't like chocolate, ice cream or even French fries. But interestingly, I haven't yet met anyone who doesn't like noodles. Udon noodles are wonderfully satisfying, and with their neutral flavor, they soak up and highlight this tasty umami sauce. This is great either hot or cold. So, no worries if you don't have the time to heat up at lunchtime.

Serves 1 to 2

6.2 oz (175 g) udon noodles

2 tbsp (28 ml) grapeseed oil

8 oz (225 g) cremini mushrooms

1 cup (71 g) broccoli florets

1 stalk celery

¼ cup (35 g) peanuts

SAUCE

¼ cup (60 ml) tamari or soy sauce

1 tbsp (15 ml) rice vinegar

1½ tsp (4 g) arrowroot starch

1 tsp (2 g) minced fresh ginger

1½ tsp (8 ml) hot sauce

1½ tsp (8 ml) pure maple syrup or agave nectar

1 clove garlic, minced

OPTIONAL TOPPINGS

Pumpkin seeds

Green onions

Red pepper flakes

Black sesame seeds

Cook the noodles according to the package instructions. Mix together the sauce ingredients in a bowl. Heat the grapeseed oil in a skillet over medium-high heat. Add all the vegetables and cook, stirring, for 2 minutes. Add the sauce and cook for another 5 minutes. Add the cooked noodles and cook, stirring, for another minute to warm the noodles. Add your desired toppings. This can be served hot or cold.

# QUICK BOK CHOY MUSHROOM SOUP

*gluten-free*

Combine all the good feelings and good intentions in the world, and you get this soup. Yes, I have strong emotions about this wonderfully aromatic, warming soup. I suggest serving with hot sauce, lime and sprouts.

## Serves 2

5 cups (1.2 L) vegetable stock or water, or a combination

2 tbsp (28 ml) olive oil

½ onion, chopped

2 cloves garlic, minced

8 oz (225 g) cremini or shiitake mushrooms, sliced

1 tsp (2 g) minced fresh ginger

3 baby bok choy, sliced

1 medium red bell pepper, seeded and finely diced

2 tbsp (28 ml) tamari (for gluten-free) or soy sauce

4 oz (115 g) gluten-free soba or udon noodles

1 tbsp (16 g) brown rice miso paste (optional)

2 tbsp (2 g) chopped fresh cilantro

Freshly ground black pepper

Place the vegetable stock in a pot and bring to a boil. At the same time, heat the olive oil in a skillet over medium-high heat, add the onion and cook, stirring, for about 5 minutes. Add the garlic, mushrooms, ginger, bok choy, bell pepper and soy sauce and cook for another 2 minutes. Break the soba noodles into small pieces and add to the boiling stock along with the miso paste. Also add the veggie mixture and let it boil for 2 minutes. Turn off the heat and add the cilantro and black pepper to taste.

# VEGETABLE GRATIN

*gluten-free*

You are either addicted to cauliflower gratin or you haven't tried it yet. Here is a quick vegan recipe that makes a head start by half-cooking the veggies in a pan to cut down on oven time. It doesn't cut down much at all in taste, though.

Serves 3

### SAUCE

1 cup (140 g) raw cashews

¼ cup (32 g) nutritional yeast

1 tbsp (15 ml) freshly squeezed lemon juice or cider vinegar

1 tsp (3 g) garlic powder

½ tsp onion powder

¼ tsp freshly ground black pepper

Salt

### THE REST

2 tbsp (28 ml) grapeseed oil

½ medium cauliflower, cut into florets

1 cup (150 g) fresh or frozen peas (thawed if frozen)

½ cup (82 g) frozen corn, thawed

2 stalks celery, chopped

1 potato, diced

1 carrot, diced

Preheat the oven to 400°F (200°C). Place all the sauce ingredients in a blender, add 1 cup (235 ml) of water and blend until you get a smooth batter. Set aside. In a cast-iron or other pan, heat the grapeseed oil over medium heat. Add the vegetables and cook, stirring, for about 10 minutes. Turn off the heat. If you used a cast-iron pan, just pour in the sauce. If you used a regular pan, transfer the veggie mixture to a deep baking dish and pour the sauce over it. Bake in the oven for 20 minutes. It is done when the potatoes are soft.

# BITE-SIZE BAKED TOFU

*gluten-free*

Tofu is one of the best protein sources available in the plant world. I feel ready for a workout just by looking at it. After all, it is a prime member of the "complete protein club," featuring the complete set of the essential amino acids our body needs. That said, I go with organic tofu, avoiding GMO soybeans. It is easy to get along with tofu; it just needs some love in the form of seasoning and it will return the favor.

Serves 2 to 3

½ cup (70 g) raw cashews

¼ cup (32 g) nutritional yeast

1 tsp (3 g) onion powder

1 tsp (3 g) garlic powder

1 tsp (2 g) freshly ground black pepper

1 tsp (2 g) dried thyme

Salt

¾ cup (96 g) arrowroot powder or cornstarch

14 oz (397 g) extra-firm tofu, cut into bite-size cubes

OPTIONAL FOR SERVING

Sprouts

Shredded red cabbage

Baby kale

Start by preheating the oven to 350°F (175°C). Put all the ingredients, except the arrowroot and tofu, and including salt to taste, in a high-speed blender, add ½ cup (120 ml) of water, and blend until smooth. Mix in the arrowroot powder and pour the batter in a wide bowl. Dip the tofu cubes in the batter, making sure they are well coated. Place the tofu cubes on a baking sheet and bake them for 40 to 50 minutes. I serve this with sprouts, shredded red cabbage and baby kale.

# BROCCOLI WALDORF SALAD

gluten-free

Not all salads are meant to be leafy. This one has a lot of texture going for it and it is a personal favorite. It works perfectly as a light meal, as a wrap filling or a side dish.

## Serves 2

SALAD

2 cup (142 g) broccoli florets, chopped

1 stalk celery, chopped

½ apple, cored and chopped

¼ red onion, chopped

⅓ cup (40 g) dried cranberries or raisins

½ cup (55 g) chopped pecans

DRESSING

½ cup (115 g) vegan mayonnaise (page 179) or vegan yogurt

Juice of ½ lemon

1½ tsp (8 ml) pure maple syrup or agave nectar

Toss together the salad ingredients in a bowl. In a separate small bowl, whisk the dressing ingredients together and pour over the salad.

# VEGETABLE PAELLA

*gluten-free*

Paella is a Valencian rice dish that is traditionally cooked in a very large pan over an open fire fueled by orange and pine branches. According to legend, this infuses the rice with the scented smoke. Paella also uses lots of meat and seafood. Neither of those are very practical for vegans. So, here is an easy vegan version that does the trick.

This paella has a seemingly infinite capacity for saffron and hot red pepper flakes. It just keeps developing a deeper and deeper taste. It's perfect for warming up the tummy and the soul.

## Serves 2 to 3

2 tbsp (28 ml) olive oil

½ onion, chopped

2 carrots, chopped

1 cup (150 g) peas

½ cup (75 g) corn

½ cup (75 g) cherry tomatoes, cut in half

½ green bell pepper, seeded and chopped

½ red bell pepper, seeded and chopped

1 clove garlic, minced

1 cup (195 g) uncooked paella or arborio rice

2 cups (475 ml) vegetable stock

1 bay leaf

A generous pinch of saffron (optional)

1 tsp dried thyme

Salt and freshly ground black pepper

Crushed red pepper flakes

¼ cup (15 g) chopped fresh parsley (optional)

In a large skillet over medium heat, heat the olive oil, add the onion and cook for a few minutes. Add the carrots, peas, corn, tomatoes, bell peppers and garlic. Lower the heat to medium-low and cook for 7 minutes.

Rinse the rice and put it in a separate pot. Add the vegetable stock and bring to a boil. Once boiling, add the bay leaf and saffron (crush the saffron with your fingertips). Combine with the vegetables that you cooked in the previous step. Add the rest of the ingredients, except the parsley, and including salt, black pepper and crushed red pepper flakes to taste, and stir. Lower the heat to very low and cover the top of the pot with foil so it makes a tight seal. After 20 minutes of cooking, remove the foil carefully. If the rice is still too moist, keep cooking, uncovered, for an additional 5 minutes. If you like, sprinkle some chopped parsley over the paella when serving.

# EASY CHILI

There are many ways to cook a nice chili, each with a different feeling. You can slow cook; you can go heavy on the spices for an intensely warming dish. Or you can try this version that's more summerlike: easy, light and colorful. It can be enjoyed hot or cold.

Serves 2 to 3

2 tbsp (28 ml) olive oil

1 onion, chopped

2 cloves garlic, chopped

1 jalapeño pepper, seeded and chopped

1 red bell pepper, seeded and chopped

1 sweet potato, cubed

1 potato, cubed

1 tomato, diced

1 cup (235 ml) vegetable stock or water

2 tbsp (32 g) tomato paste

¼ tsp red pepper flakes

¼ tsp grated fresh ginger

1 bay leaf

¾ cup (150 g) dried beans (soaked overnight and boiled until tender), or 1 (15-oz [425-g]) can beans, drained and rinsed

FOR SERVING

Cooked rice

Chopped fresh parsley

Heat the olive oil in a large skillet over medium heat. Add the onion and garlic. Cook until onion turns translucent, about 5 minutes. Add the rest of the ingredients, except the beans, rice and parsley, and stir. Cook until the potatoes are soft, 20 to 25 minutes. Add the beans, cook for a few more minutes and serve with the rice and parsley.

# GREEN LENTIL AND SWEET POTATO SOUP

gluten-free

I am totally a soup person and I can't have enough of it, especially a spicy one with a deep warmth like this. It is easy enough to just jar it and take it to work for lunch, perhaps alongside some bread or rice. But it is also not uncommon for me to have soup for breakfast.

Serves 2 to 3

2 tbsp (28 ml) olive oil

1 medium onion, diced

2 to 3 cloves garlic, minced

1 tsp (3 g) ground cumin

1 tsp (2 g) sweet curry powder

1 tsp (2 g) freshly ground black pepper

¼ tsp cayenne pepper

¾ cup (144 g) dried green lentils

1 large sweet potato, diced

5 cups (1.2 L) vegetable stock or water

1 bay leaf

2 cups (142 g) sliced kale (sliced into ribbons)

¼ cup (60 ml) coconut cream

¼ cup (32 g) nutritional yeast

1 tsp (3 g) grated fresh ginger

Salt

Heat the olive oil in a pot over medium heat. Add the onion and garlic and cook, stirring, for about 3 minutes, then add the spices and cook for 3 more minutes. Rinse the lentils. Add the lentils and sweet potato to the pan and stir a few times, then add the vegetable stock and bay leaf. Bring to a boil and lower the heat to low. Simmer, with the lid on, for about 20 minutes or until the lentils are softened. Add the rest of the ingredients, adding salt to taste and cook, stirring, for 5 more minutes. Serve hot.

# ROASTED EGGPLANT SALAD

gluten-free

Eggplant, roasted with skin on, develops a rich and smoky flavor that works really well in a variety of dishes. I like mixing it up with other roasted and fresh vegetables and making a delicious salad to go on toast. This salad will keep in the fridge nicely for a few days, so you can keep coming for more.

Serves 2

1 large eggplant

1 red bell pepper

1 green bell pepper

1 shallot

1 cup (60 g) chopped fresh parsley

1 tsp (3 g) garlic powder, or 1 clove garlic, minced

Juice of ½ lemon

1 tbsp (15 ml) olive oil

1 tbsp (2 g) za'atar (or a mix of sumac, thyme and toasted sesame seeds)

Salt

Barbecue the eggplant and the red bell pepper with the skin on: Poke the eggplant a few times with a knife and place along with the bell pepper on a hot grill. Cook until the pepper skin is moderately charred. The eggplant, depending on size, may take longer and it will take the heat so place it on the hottest spot and be patient until it gets all mushy. Alternatively, you can roast them both in the oven. Cut the eggplant in half lengthwise and make a pattern of knife cuts on the flesh to aid in faster cooking. Roast the eggplant and the bell peppers at 450°F (230°C), for about 20 minutes, or until the eggplant is fully mushy and the pepper skins are moderately charred. When done, peel off the eggplant skin and optionally the pepper skins. Mash the eggplant with a fork and chop the bell peppers and the shallot. Mix together all the remaining ingredients, adding salt to taste. Serve chilled, as a salad or on toast.

# RED LENTIL DHAL

gluten-free

One of the best things about red lentils, apart from their supernutrition, is that they cook fast. So they are the perfect base for a filling, yummy meal. A prime example is this wonderfully spicy dhal. I love having this along with a side of brown rice.

Serves 2 to 3

1 cup (192 g) dried red lentils

2 tbsp (28 ml) coconut or olive oil

½ red onion, chopped

2 cloves garlic

1 tbsp (2 g) grated fresh ginger

½ cup (90 g) chopped tomato

¼ cup (60 ml) coconut cream

1 tbsp (6 g) curry powder

1 tsp (3 g) ground cumin

½ tsp ground coriander

¼ tsp cayenne pepper

Salt and freshly ground black pepper

OPTIONAL

3 tbsp (3 g) chopped fresh cilantro

1 tbsp (15 ml) freshly squeezed lime juice

Boil the red lentils in 4 cups (946 ml) of water and a bit of salt, for about 15 minutes.

Heat the coconut oil in a pot, add the onion and cook, stirring, for 5 minutes. Add ½ cup (120 ml) of water and the rest of the ingredients, except the cilantro and lime juice, and including salt and black pepper to taste, and continue to cook, stirring, for another 10 minutes. Adjust the salt and add the cilantro and lime juice before serving, if desired.

# ZUCCHINI BOATS

gluten-free

This is an interesting and fun way to cook zucchini into a delicious lunch with minimal effort. The zucchini stays a little firm in this recipe, and I absolutely love that fresher feeling and texture.

## Serves 2

¼ cup (35 g) raw cashews

3 tbsp (24 g) nutritional yeast

½ tsp garlic powder

2 tbsp (28 ml) cider vinegar

1 tbsp (9 g) capers

½ cup (115 g) vegan mayonnaise (page 179)

Salt and freshly ground black pepper

2 zucchini

Preheat the oven to 350°F (175°C).

Put the cashews, nutritional yeast and garlic powder in a food processor and grind until you get a fine-grain mixture. Add the cider vinegar, capers, mayo, salt and pepper to taste. Pulse the food processor a few times to mix them in.

Cut the zucchini in half lengthwise and lay them on a sheet of parchment paper or a baking sheet, skin side down. Spread the filling over the zucchini halves and bake, uncovered, for 15 to 20 minutes, or until the filling starts brown.

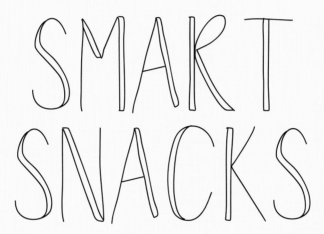

# SMART SNACKS

Who is to say that the day is to be made of three meals straight? I want snacks. I could even skip some of my meals in favor of munching on things here and there. And I don't want to have to resort to bagged, likely stale junk treats. So, I almost always have something at the ready to snack on, such as frozen snack bars, mini desserts, dips and spreads that can keep in the fridge for a while. A few of my favorites are here in this little collection.

# CRUNCH TIME CHOCOLATE CRISPIES

*gluten-free*

I would say this one is all about texture, if it wasn't also so incredibly delicious. It's the perfect frozen chocolatey nutty dessert snack with a crunch. And it takes little effort, no cooking involved.

## Makes about 6 bars

½ cup (120 ml) coconut oil, melted

2 tbsp (32 g) peanut butter

¼ cup (60 ml) pure maple syrup

1 tsp (5 ml) pure vanilla extract

¼ cup (28 g) cacao powder

Pinch of salt

¼ cup (35 g) chopped pistachios

¾ cup (16 g) crisp rice cereal (gluten-free, if necessary)

OPTIONAL TOPPINGS

¼ cup (30 g) dried cranberries, sliced in half

¼ cup (30 g) cacao nibs

Line a small baking pan, about 5 x 7-inches (13 x 18-cm), with parchment paper. Place the melted coconut oil and peanut butter in a big bowl and mix well. Add the maple syrup, vanilla, cacao powder and salt and mix again. Finally, add the pistachios and rice cereal and mix. Pour into the prepared dish. Add the toppings, if desired. Keep in the freezer for at least 4 hours. Slice into bars and serve.

EATING INSTRUCTIONS

Step 1. Pick up with your fingers and eat.

Step 2. Lick your fingers clean, or alternatively, have your fingers licked. Just saying.

# MINI LEMON CURD TARTS

*gluten-free*

You can drown all your sorrows in lemon curd. This vegan version is wonderfully fragrant and creamy smooth. In the form of individually sized mini tarts, these are kept in the freezer, available to grab when the occasion calls for it.

Makes about 4 mini tarts

## CRUST

½ cup (67 g) hazelnuts

½ cup (75 g) raisins

Pinch of salt

## FILLING

¾ cup (105 g) raw cashews

⅓ cup (75 ml) freshly squeezed lemon juice

¼ cup (60 ml) pure maple syrup

Zest of 2 lemons

1 tbsp (15 ml) coconut oil

1 tsp (5 ml) Cointreau liqueur (optional)

Pinch of turmeric (for color; optional)

Pinch of salt

## TOPPING

Fresh berries

Grind all the crust ingredients in a food processor until you get a sticky paste. Roll out the paste between 2 sheets of parchment paper to a scant ¼-inch (5-mm) thickness. Cut out 4 disks and place on the bottom of four 3-inch (7.5-cm) tart molds. Put the molds in the freezer and move on to make the filling.

Put all the filling ingredients in a high-speed blender and blend until smooth. Pour the filling over the crust in the tart molds. Place back in the freezer and wait for at least 4 hours. Top with berries and serve either immediately or after a bit of thawing, depending on your preference.

# JUST BECAUSE CARROT CAKE BARS

*gluten-free*

It is always a joy to take a carrot bar from the freezer and plunge into an instant fall feeling. No flour in this one, as it is made with the vegan "cheesecake" method. The crust, however, is not raw.

Makes about 6 bars

CRUST

½ cup (55 g) pecans or walnuts

½ cup (75 g) raisins

2 tbsp (28 ml) pure maple syrup

1 tbsp (15 ml) coconut oil

4 medium carrots, grated

1 tsp (3 g) ground cinnamon

⅛ tsp ground cloves

FILLING

1 cup (140 g) raw cashews (soaked in water for at least 4 hours and drained)

Juice and zest of 1 orange

¼ cup (60 ml) almond milk

¼ cup (60 ml) pure maple syrup

1 tsp (5 ml) pure vanilla extract

TOPPING

½ cup (70 g) roughly chopped pistachios

To make the crust, start by chopping the pecans and raisins in a food processor together with the maple syrup. You will get a sticky consistency but stop way before it turns into a smooth paste. You want to keep some texture. Set this part aside.

Heat the coconut oil in a pan over medium-low heat and cook the carrots and the crust spices together until the carrots soften, 5 to 7 minutes. Turn off the heat and combine with the pecan mixture.

Lay the crust in a small baking pan, about 5 x 7-inches (13 x 18-cm), lined with parchment paper. Blend all the filling ingredients in a high-speed blender and pour over the crust. Top with the chopped pistachios. Place the pan in the freezer. You can enjoy this frozen or you can let it thaw for about 30 minutes or more for a softer, creamy dessert.

# RAW APPLE PIE BARS

gluten-free

A classic apple pie is a lot of things, but I wouldn't quite call it refreshing or easy. Here is a twist to incorporate that wonderful apple pie feeling into a cool, refreshing and nutritious snack or a dessert option for lunch.

Makes about 6 bars

### CRUST LAYER

½ cup (55 g) pecans (optionally roasted)

¾ cup (110 g) raisins

Pinch of salt

### TOP LAYER

1 cup (140 g) raw cashews

¼ cup (60 ml) cold-pressed fresh apple juice

¼ cup (60 ml) pure maple syrup

1 tsp (5 ml) pure vanilla extract

1 tsp (5 g) ground cinnamon

¼ tsp ground nutmeg

Pinch of salt

¼ cup (60 ml) almond milk

1 tbsp (15 ml) coconut oil

Apple slices (optional), for garnish

Put all the crust layer ingredients in a food processor and process until it starts to have a sticky consistency—but make sure you stop well before it turns into a smooth paste, as the nutty texture in the crust is really nice to keep. Transfer the crust dough to a piece of parchment paper and flatten it into a 5 x 7-inch (13 x 18-cm) rectangle. You can use another piece of parchment paper on top to help roll it out. Transfer the crust, together with the bottom parchment paper, to a small baking pan, about 5 x 7-inches (13 x 18-cm), and put it in the freezer.

In the meantime, mix all the top layer ingredients in a high-speed blender until smooth. Take the crust out of the freezer briefly and pour the top layer mixture evenly over the crust. Cover and keep in the freezer. Before serving, allow it to thaw at room temperature for 10 to 30 minutes, depending on how creamy you like it. Garnish with apple slices.

# MATCHA NANA ICE CREAM

*gluten-free*

In the world of plant-based cuisine, you can make ice cream with one, and only one, ingredient: bananas. And it is brilliant, though it does get better with a few more additions, such as peanut butter and matcha green tea! This ice cream is a favorite because it is a delicious, easy and invigorating superfood that I am happy to eat anytime.

Serves 1 to 2

2 frozen bananas, peeled and thickly sliced

1½ tsp (8 g) peanut butter (or any nut butter)

1½ tsp (8 ml) pure maple syrup

½ tsp matcha tea powder

OPTIONAL TOPPINGS

Berries

Hazelnuts

Cacao nibs

Put all the ingredients, except the toppings, in a food processor and blend until the mixture reaches an ice cream consistency. Top with berries, hazelnuts and cacao nibs, if you wish. Serve immediately.

# CAULIFLOWER DIP

gluten-free

This is a great warm-serve dip that nicely balances the earthy and hearty flavor with a cheesy flavor and a hint of sourness. It is definitely a pleaser, too, if you want to serve as an appetizer to guests.

## Makes 3 cups (360 g) dip

1 medium cauliflower

2 tbsp (28 ml) olive oil

1 tsp (2 g) dried thyme

Salt and freshly ground black pepper

SAUCE

1 cup (140 g) raw cashews

1 cup (235 ml) almond milk

¼ cup (32 g) nutritional yeast

1 tsp (3 g) garlic powder

1 tbsp (15 ml) cider vinegar

1 tbsp (9 g) capers

Salt and freshly ground black pepper

Set the oven to 400°F (200°C). Cut the cauliflower into florets and place in a baking pan. Coat with the olive oil, thyme and salt and pepper to taste. Cook for 15 to 20 minutes. In the meantime, blend all the sauce ingredients, including salt and pepper to taste, in a high-speed blender. Transfer the roasted cauliflower to a saucepan, pour the sauce over it and cook for 5 to 7 minutes over medium heat. Serve warm or at room temperature.

# PICKLED BEETS

*gluten-free*

I almost always have these pickled beets in my fridge because they work so well with everything savory: sandwiches and salads, of course, but also as a side to other veggie dishes, pastas and rice.

Makes about 2½ cups (560 g) beets

3 medium beets

¼ cup (60 ml) cider vinegar

1½ tsp (9 g) salt

½ tsp dried thyme

Wash the beets and boil them in 5 cups (1.2 L) of water until they soften. Save 1 cup (235 ml) of the cooking liquid as beet juice. An easy way to peel off the beet skins is to wrap the beets in paper towel, twist and shear. Peel and slice the beets (or cube them), and put them in a jar together with the rest of the ingredients and the reserved cup of the beet juice. Close the lid and chill in the fridge for 1 to 2 days before serving. It will keep in the fridge for up to 4 weeks.

# ZUCCHINI CARROT SPREAD

*gluten-free*

This might just make you reevaluate what you think about carrots and zucchini, in a good way. You know how some recipes take a few ingredients and totally transform them to create an entirely new experience? This is one of them. It will happily work as a stand-alone snack, a side dish, a sandwich filling or a bruschetta topping.

Makes about 2 cups (480 g) spread

### SAUCE

½ cup (70 g) raw cashews

¼ cup (32 g) nutritional yeast

1 tsp (2 g) freshly ground black pepper

1 tsp (3 g) garlic powder

¼ cup (60 ml) cider vinegar

Salt

### THE REST

1 medium carrot, chopped or grated

1 medium zucchini, chopped or grated

2 tbsp (28 ml) olive oil

¼ cup (16 g) chopped fresh dill

¼ cup (60 g) chopped fresh parsley

¼ cup (28 g) roughly chopped pecans

Place all the sauce ingredients, plus ½ cup (120 ml) of water, in a high-speed blender and blend until smooth.

You can grate the carrots or zucchini or chop them finely in a food processor. Heat the olive oil in a skillet over medium-low heat. Add the carrots and zucchini and cook until they lose their water, 10 to 15 minutes, stirring occasionally. Add the sauce and cook for another 2 minutes.

Transfer to a storage container with a cover and let cool uncovered. When at room temperature, add the dill, parsley and pecans. It will keep in the fridge, covered, for up to 3 days.

# BEET HUMMUS

*gluten-free*

Beet hummus is basically color and fun added to an already nearly perfect hummus. It's a little more nutritious, too.

Makes about 2 cups (490 g) hummus

1 cup (240 g) cooked or canned chickpeas

1 large beet, cooked and peeled

3 tbsp (45 ml) olive oil

2 tbsp (30 g) tahini

3 cloves garlic, crushed

1 tsp (3 g) ground cumin

½ tsp freshly ground black pepper

Juice and zest of 1 lemon

Salt

Process all the ingredients, plus 3 tablespoons (45 ml) of water and salt to taste, in a food processor, adjusting the texture to your liking. If you like your hummus very smooth and creamy, you can use a high-speed blender instead. This will keep in the fridge for up to a week.

# MUHAMMARA

gluten-free

This little-known gem, drawn from Mediterranean cuisine, is an instant hit every time I serve it. It is a relatively simple red bell pepper spread (or dip) that has a strikingly intense, savory umami flavor.

Makes about 1 ½ cups (270 g) muhammara

2 tbsp (28 ml) olive oil

2 red bell peppers, seeded and chopped

½ cup (130 g) tomato paste

Salt and freshly ground black pepper

2 cloves garlic, minced

¼ cup (30 g) chopped walnuts

Heat the olive oil in a pan over medium heat and cook the red bell peppers for about 10 minutes. Add the tomato paste and salt and black pepper to taste and cook for 1 to 2 more minutes, spreading the tomato paste evenly and adjusting the salt. Put this mixture in a food processor along with minced garlic and pulse until you get a moderately textured but uniform spread. Transfer to a bowl or a storage container, then mix in the chopped walnuts. Let cool and serve at room temperature. This will keep in the fridge for a few days.

# SPINACH MUSHROOM PROTEIN DIP

How cool is it when you are treating your taste buds and your body at the same time? This is a warm serve dip with a luscious, engulfing flavor. The sauce blends in tofu, which lends a good amount of protein and a creamy smooth consistency to it.

Makes about 2 cups (240 g) dip

SAUCE

8 oz (225 g) firm tofu

1 tsp (3 g) dry mustard

1 tbsp (15 ml) soy sauce

3 tbsp (24 g) nutritional yeast

1 tsp (3 g) arrowroot starch

1 tsp (3 g) garlic powder

½ tsp smoked paprika

1 tsp (2 g) freshly ground black pepper

½ tsp dried thyme

1 tbsp (4 g) chopped fresh dill

1 tbsp (6 g) chopped fresh mint

THE REST

1 tbsp (15 ml) grapeseed oil or other vegetable oil

½ medium onion, chopped

1 cup (30 g) sliced spinach

2 cups (140 g) sliced mushrooms

1 tbsp (3 g) sun-dried tomatoes

Place the sauce ingredients, plus ¾ cup (175 ml) of water, in a blender and blend until smooth. Set aside.

Heat the oil in a pan over medium heat. Add the onion and cook for 3 to 5 minutes, or until the onions start to turn translucent. Add the spinach and cook for another 3 minutes. Add the mushrooms together with the sun-dried tomatoes and cook until the mushrooms are browned and tender, about 5 minutes. Add the sauce and cook until the sauce thickens, 3 to 5 minutes. Serve warm.

# BASICS

Sauces, condiments, garnishes, plant-based cheese spreads and sweet creams: these rule the kitchen. They are the ultimate in versatility, they often show up in recipes and hold the power to turn the bland into exciting. Having a few of these at the ready just makes life so much easier and tastier.

# COCONUT WHIPPED CREAM

gluten-free

This is a wonderful option for the cream component in vegan desserts, for dipping berries in, or for topping hot drinks or smoothies. Use it anywhere one might imagine using traditional whipped cream.

Makes about ¾ cup (175 ml) whipped cream

¾ cup (175 ml) full-fat coconut milk

2½ tbsp (40 ml) pure maple syrup

1 tsp (5 ml) pure vanilla extract

2 tsp (10 ml) freshly squeezed lemon juice

Blend all the ingredients in a blender.

# FRESH CRANBERRY ORANGE RELISH

gluten-free

This relish is incredibly simple, with only three ingredients and no cooking. It will work nicely in sandwiches, of course, but also as a side (I'm thinking a vegetable gratin, for example). It will also transform your tofu.

Makes about 2 cups (480 g) relish

1 orange, peeled and cut into pieces

8 oz (225 g) fresh cranberries

¼ cup (60 ml) pure maple syrup

Put the orange pieces, cranberries and maple syrup in a food processor and grind until you get an evenly textured mix. Keep refrigerated.

# CUSTARD CREAM

gluten-free

Vegan custard is as easy as four ingredients and a blender. Besides all the places one would use custard (vegan donut filling!?), this is also perfect for overnight oats, parfaits or dipping fruits and cookies.

Makes about 2 cups (400 g) cream

¾ cup (105 g) raw cashews

¾ cup (175 ml) full-fat coconut milk

⅓ cup (80 ml) pure maple syrup

1 tsp (5 ml) pure vanilla extract

Blend all the ingredients in a high-speed blender. Let it wait in the fridge for at least 4 hours or overnight, before serving.

# KALE MINT PESTO

*gluten-free*

Pesto hardly needs any introduction. Feel free to go nuts and spread this all over your pasta, homemade pesto pizzas (!), sandwiches, toast ... One variation: You can try using chard instead of kale.

Makes about 2 cups (520 g) pesto

3 cloves garlic

¾ cup (105 g) raw cashews

¼ cup (42 g) hemp seeds

¼ cup (32 g) nutritional yeast

¼ tsp freshly ground black pepper

Red pepper flakes (optional)

3 cups (201 g) chopped kale (about 1 small bunch)

¼ cup (7 g) fresh mint leaves

Juice of 1 lemon

Sea salt

¼ cup (60 ml) olive oil, plus more if desired

Mix all the ingredients, except the salt and olive oil, in a food processor. Add sea salt to taste and the olive oil and pulse a few more times to combine.

# LUNCH SAVER EGGPLANT CASHEW SAUCE

gluten-free

Excellent as a pasta sauce, or to lay sautéed mushrooms over, or to use as a sauce for open-faced sandwiches ...

Makes about 1 ½ cups (375 g) sauce

1 eggplant

½ cup (70 g) raw cashews

Juice of ½ lemon

¼ tsp freshly ground black pepper

2 cloves garlic

2 tbsp (16 g) nutritional yeast

1 tbsp (15 ml) olive oil

The eggplant can be oven roasted, grilled on the barbecue or directly over the stovetop (this last one is a little messy, but it works). In either case, keep the skin on, poke a few knife holes in the eggplant and roast until it is really mushy. Make sure to not undercook it.

Blend all the ingredients, except the olive oil and eggplant, in a high-speed blender. Heat the olive oil in a saucepan over medium heat. Add the eggplant and the blended mixture and cook for about 5 minutes.

# HOT TAHINI CURRY SAUCE

*gluten-free*

You can never have enough sauces in your arsenal. Wield the power to transform a bunch of veggies into a yummy lunch. It can also be used with pasta or salads, or as a spread.

## Makes 1 cup (250 g) sauce

⅓ cup (80 g) tahini

Juice of 1 lemon

2 tbsp (28 ml) tamari (for gluten-free) or soy sauce

1 tbsp (2 g) sweet curry powder

1 tsp (5 ml) hot sauce

1 tsp (3 g) garlic powder

1 tsp (5 ml) pure maple syrup or agave syrup

Freshly ground black pepper

Mix together all the ingredients in a bowl, adding ¼ to ½ cup (60 to 120 ml) of water according to how you prefer the consistency of the sauce. It can stay in the fridge for up to a week.

# PEANUT BUTTER CURRY SAUCE

*gluten-free*

A handy sauce to keep at the ready. It can be used as a salad dressing, sandwich spread or veggie seasoning and it can turn bland things into interesting really fast.

Makes about ¾ cup (175 ml) sauce

3 tbsp (48 g) peanut butter

1½ tsp (3 g) curry powder

1 tsp (5 ml) pure maple syrup

1 tbsp (15 ml) tamari (for gluten-free) or soy sauce

Juice of ½ lime

⅛ tsp cayenne pepper (optional, if you like hot)

1 clove garlic, minced

1½ tsp (4 g) grated fresh ginger

Mix everything together, adding ¼ cup (60 ml) or more of water, until your desired consistency is reached.

# OMG FRESH DILL CHEESE

*gluten-free*

I really debated calling this the "Dreamy Cheese" since that would have been really descriptive. This is one easy plant-based cheese that just keeps getting better every day it stays in the fridge. It will keep for a week. It will not goo and stretch—it's just not that kind—but it will not disappoint when cooked. I had one of the best grilled cheese sandwiches (in a sesame seed bagel!) with this cheese. It can also be used in soups.

Makes about 1 ½ cups (200 g) cheese

1 cup (140 g) raw cashews

3 tbsp (24 g) nutritional yeast

¼ tsp freshly ground black pepper

½ tsp salt

¼ cup (60 ml) cider vinegar

½ tsp garlic powder

1 tbsp (4 g) finely chopped fresh dill

Put everything, except the dill, in a high-speed blender. Add ¼ cup (60 ml) of water and blend until smooth. Transfer to a bowl and mix in the dill. Cover and let sit at room temperature for 1 to 2 hours. Place in the fridge and let it chill overnight.

# MISO CHEESE SPREAD

gluten-free

Incredible cheesy spreads are surprisingly easy to achieve with plants. Plus you get that certain satisfaction from dabbling in the fine art of cheese making. This goes really well in bagels and even grilled cheese sandwiches.

Makes about 1 ½ cups (188 g) spread

1 cup (140 g) raw cashews

2 tbsp (32 g) white miso

2 tbsp (16 g) nutritional yeast

1 tsp (3 g) garlic powder

¼ tsp freshly ground black pepper

¼ tsp dried thyme

⅓ cup (80 ml) cider vinegar or water

Blend all the ingredients in a high-speed blender until smooth. Transfer to a container with lid and let sit at room temperature for 1 to 2 hours. Chill it in the fridge overnight before serving. It will keep in the fridge for up to a week.

# MUSTARD

gluten-free

Whole-grain mustard is an absolute favorite of mine, as far as condiments go. I am much more comfortable consuming something frequently if I made it at home, since I know I am using fresh, healthy, high-quality ingredients, and I can tweak the taste exactly to my liking. And it keeps in the fridge for about three months, so the little time it takes to make this is time very well spent.

Makes about 1 cup (175 ml) mustard

½ cup (120 ml) dry white wine

¼ cup (60 ml) cider vinegar

¼ cup (43 g) brown mustard seeds

¼ cup (43 g) yellow mustard seeds

½ tsp kosher salt

Mix all the ingredients in a bowl. Cover with plastic wrap and let sit at room temperature for 2 days. After 2 days, blend the mixture in a blender. Note that you will still have some texture left. This will keep in the fridge for up to 3 months.

# TOMATO CONFIT

gluten-free

Having a few garnishes like this at the ready makes snacking and meals so much easier and tastier. I am very fond of tomatoes, and I often use this confit in salads, pasta sauces, bruschettas, pizza toppings and pretty much anywhere a rich tomato flavor and a Mediterranean feeling is called for.

Makes about 1 ½ cups (270 g) confit

16 oz (455 g) mixed cherry tomatoes, cut in half lengthwise

3 cloves garlic, chopped

3 sprigs fresh rosemary

Salt and freshly ground black pepper

¼ cup (60 ml) olive oil

Preheat the oven to 350°F (175°C). Put the tomatoes, garlic and rosemary on a baking sheet and cover the top with foil. Bake for 40 to 45 minutes, remove from the oven and let cool. Transfer to a jar, sprinkle with salt and pepper to taste and add the olive oil. It will keep it in the fridge, covered, for several weeks.

# RED BELL PEPPER AIOLI

gluten-free

This one is actually made up of two recipes. One for a vegan mayonnaise and another for making the aioli. Feel free to replace the first one with a store-bought vegan mayo, if you'd like. The red pepper aioli just enriches and flavors the mayo so it is complete and delicious. I use this on grilled sandwiches (spread on the aioli after cooking the sandwich), over oven-roasted potatoes, over corn bread or as a salad dressing.

Makes 1 ½ cups (337 g) mayo and ¾ cup (175 g) aioli

## VEGAN MAYONNAISE

¼ cup (60 ml) unsweetened soy milk

1 tbsp (15 ml) cider vinegar

1 tbsp (15 ml) freshly squeezed lemon juice

½ tsp pure maple syrup or agave nectar

1 tsp (2 g) freshly ground white pepper (optional)

¼ tsp dry mustard, or ½ tsp Dijon mustard

1 tsp (6 g) salt

1 cup (235 ml) grapeseed oil

## RED BELL PEPPER AIOLI

½ cup (90 g) chopped roasted red peppers

⅓ cup (75 g) vegan mayonnaise (store-bought or use above recipe)

1 tsp (3 g) garlic powder

Salt and freshly ground black pepper

## VEGAN MAYONNAISE

Blend all the mayonnaise ingredients, except the grapeseed oil, in a food processor until smooth. Slowly stir in the oil.

## RED BELL PEPPER AIOLI

Blend all the aioli ingredients, including salt and black pepper to taste, in a food processor until smooth. It can last in the fridge for up to 1 week.

# ACKNOWLEDGMENTS

So much help, love, encouragement, criticism and inspiration went toward this book's realization that it is next to impossible to individually address and acknowledge all. I will begin by thanking my blog readers and Instagram peeps. The whole reason that I am doing any of this is to share with you, inspire you and get inspired by you. And any success I may have attained, I owe wholly to your feedback. I thank you, Emre, my love, for being right next to me every step of the way, lending your rock-solid support through the ebbs and flows. And for your unyielding determination in eating everything. My son, Arel, you had to be patient through the hard work put into this book; thank you for being such a cool guy about it. Thank you for taking pride in what we do and being part of it as my avid food critic. Thank you, Emily von Euw, of *This Rawsome Vegan Life*, for the support when it was most needed. And thank you, Page Street Publishing, and in particular, Marissa, for believing in my work and making me feel like I'm in very good hands at all times.

# ABOUT THE AUTHOR

Maya Sozer is a culinary creative and a photographer who is obsessed with kinder, plant-based food and driven with her immense love for the planet and all of its inhabitants. She draws inspiration from her Mediterranean roots as well as world cuisine, often fusing the two. Her recipes are guided both by her professional experience as a chef and her longtime commitment to healthy home cooking. Maya comes from a diverse background in visual arts that she now draws upon for her food styling and photography. She is the creator of the *Dreamy Leaf* blog. She now lives in Charlotte, North Carolina, with her family and when she is not cooking, she loves running, doing yoga and being outdoors.

# INDEX